**insight text guide**

Niki Cook

# Growing up Asian in Australia

Edited by Alice Pung

First published in 2021, reprinted in 2022.

Insight Publications Pty Ltd
3/350 Charman Road
Cheltenham VIC 3192
Australia
Tel: +61 3 8571 4950
Fax: +61 3 8571 0257
Email: books@insightpublications.com.au

**www.insightpublications.com.au**

A catalogue record for this book is available from the National Library of Australia

*Alice Pung's Growing up Asian in Australia* / Niki Cook

Niki Cook asserts the moral right to be identified as the author of this work.

ISBNs:
9781922525437 (print)
9781922525444 (digital)
9781922525451 (bundle: print + digital)

Cover design by Gisela Beer

Printed by Markono Print Media Pte Ltd

# contents

# CHARACTER MAP

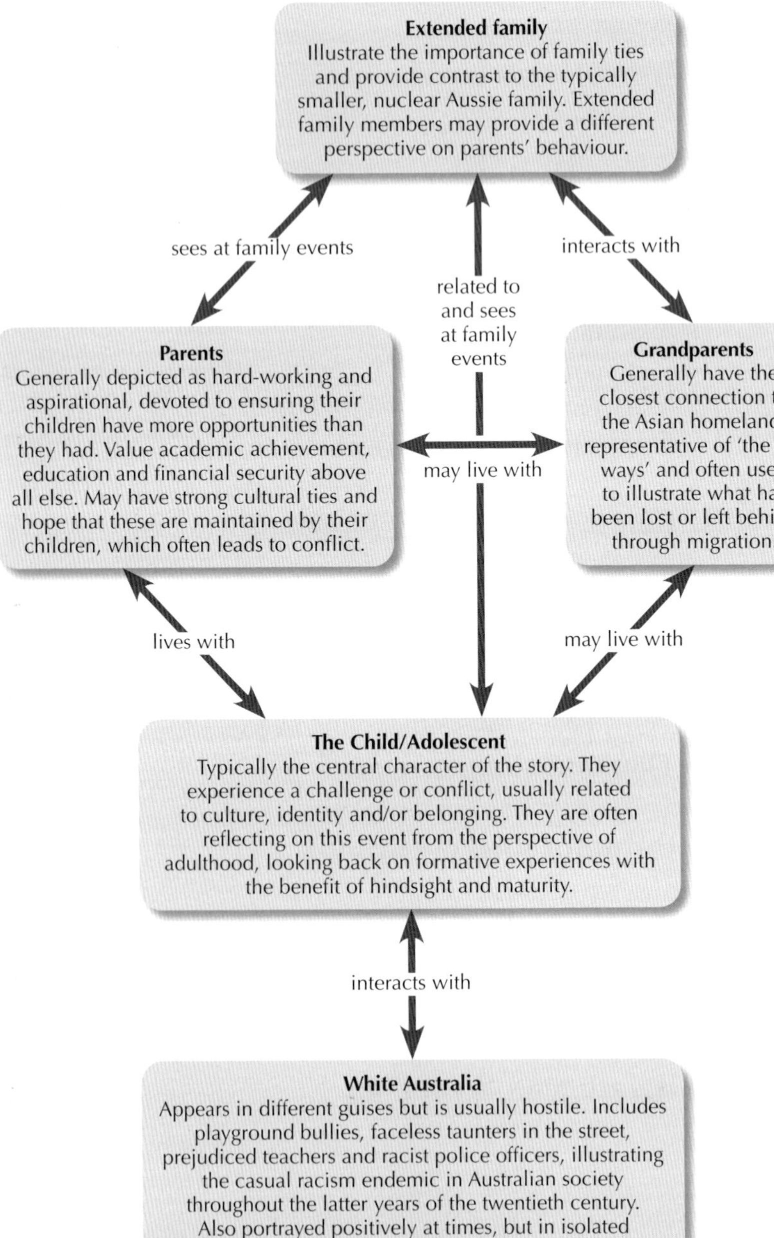

# OVERVIEW

## About the editor

Born in 1981 in Footscray, a western suburb of Melbourne, Victoria, Alice Pung was the first child of ethnic Chinese parents who fled the Killing Fields of Pol Pot's regime in Cambodia. Having walked across Cambodia and Vietnam to reach a Thai refugee camp, her parents and grandmother arrived in Melbourne as refugee migrants in 1980. Her father named her after the title character in *Alice in Wonderland*, in celebration of the opportunities afforded to them by their new life in Australia. Pung grew up in the western suburbs of Melbourne, with her parents, grandmother and three younger siblings. Her father ran a Retravision store (a chain of stores that sells electrical products and home appliances) and her mother worked as a goldsmith, both labouring hard to succeed and provide for their family in their new adopted country. As was expected in her traditional Chinese family, Pung looked after her younger siblings and the house, while also keeping up with her studies. Despite suffering from depression in her later school years, she performed well in her VCE studies, and went on to study law at the University of Melbourne.

Pung's first book, *Unpolished Gem* (2006), is a memoir recounting her experiences of childhood and adolescence as an Asian Australian, interwoven with stories of her parents' and grandmother's lives in Cambodia. It won the 2007 Australian Book Industry Newcomer of the Year Award and was shortlisted for several other awards. Her follow-up, *Her Father's Daughter* (2013), continued her exploration of autobiographical material, focusing more on her father's experience, alongside recollections of her life in her twenties. It won the 2011 Non-Fiction Prize at the Western Australian Premier's Book Awards, and was shortlisted for awards in a number of other states. In 2014 Pung published her first novel, *Laurinda*, and in 2021 she published her second, *One Hundred Days*. She has also written several books featuring the character of Marly for the *Our Australian Girl* series.

Having studied at the University of Melbourne after her high-school studies, Pung continues to work at the university as its Artist in Residence. Outside of her literary work, she is a qualified lawyer and a practising solicitor.

Pung's work is heavily influenced by her experiences as an Asian Australian, and in *Growing up Asian in Australia* she has collated an anthology that reflects the shared experiences of a range of other Asian Australian writers.

## Synopsis

Although Pung's anthology features a wide array of text types and experiences, the overall theme is summarised effectively in the title: *Growing up Asian in Australia*. Featuring material by sixty contributors, the anthology explores the personal experiences of the writers and their family members as predominantly first- and second-generation migrants trying to find their place in an often hostile Australian society.

### Introduction

Editor Alice Pung introduces the key themes of the text and explains her motivation in compiling the anthology. She also introduces some of the universal milestones of growing up and the 'firsts' that everyone encounters during adolescence, highlighting that, while this text explores the Asian Australian experience, there are aspects of every story that will be familiar to any reader. Although the introduction is the only text written by Pung in the collection, it does an important job of framing and contextualising the content to follow.

### Strine

The stories in this section focus on language and the challenges associated with it. There is discussion of the difficulties encountered by first-generation migrants due to a lack of familiarity with English, and the reluctance of second-generation migrants to engage with the language of their parents and grandparents. The writers explore communication breakdown and the lack of understanding – both linguistically and on a deeper level – that can eventuate due to the absence of a shared tongue.

### Pioneers

This section focuses on first-generation migrants, and the challenges of adapting to a country and a culture often far removed from the one left behind. The texts in this section vary considerably in temporal setting (the place and time in which a story unfolds), ranging from Ken Chau's poem about nineteenth-century early settlers to more recent experiences of migration towards the end of the twentieth century.

### Battlers

Named for the quintessential Aussie archetype, this section focuses on the hard work of those seeking to establish lives in an often hostile environment. Battlers are those who persevere despite adversity, who struggle to survive but don't give up. Separated from others who share the same cultural background and language, for the battlers in this anthology the challenges of settling in and establishing themselves are often magnified.

### Mates

This section focuses on school experiences and the people associated with those times – the friends, the teachers and the bullies. The stories explore the learning that takes place both inside the classroom and out, as the writers reflect on the importance of social education and finding a sense of belonging. The writers recount the challenges they encountered; negotiating casual racism, the pressures of expected academic success, and the desire to fit in and connect all feature prominently.

### The Folks

The stories in this section deal with the relationships between parents and children, and the intergenerational conflict that often results from a clash of values between Asian-born parents and their Australian-raised offspring. The majority of accounts feature adults looking back at their childhood relationship with their parents, bringing the benefit of hindsight; however, there is also a story from the perspective of a parent reflecting on their relationship with their child. The understanding of both the fallibility and mortality of one's parents that comes with maturity is explored in this section as well.

### The Clan

This section widens the scope of the previous one, looking at the role of the extended family. The impact of ever-present extended family, the challenges of family gatherings, and the minefield of customs, expected behaviour and required generational respect are explored, and many authors emphasise the differences in their lives from those of their white Australian peers.

### Legends

The writers of the stories in this section explore the childhood role models, icons and idols they admired during their formative years. These range from Hong Kong cinema stars to superheroes to their own parents. The stories emphasise the importance of having someone to look up to and admire during one's formative years.

### The Hots

The formation of a sexual identity and the experience of first love are familiar parts of growing up. The stories in this section explore the challenges the writers faced in reconciling their own sexual awakening with the expectations of their family and culture. Both male and female experiences are included, highlighting the contrasting gendered expectations regarding sexual expression, particularly in relation to ideas of virility and virginity. Several stories also explore the challenges the writers faced regarding their homosexuality, and the prejudices this exposed them to both within and beyond their cultural background.

### UnAustralian?

These stories focus on identity and race, and the struggle to reconcile one's internal feelings with one's outward appearance as well as to navigate the responses of others. As is clear in several of the stories in this section, even those who consider themselves Australian are still subject to prejudice and stereotyping, and must battle pre-existing views and assumptions made about them.

### Tall Poppies

In contrast to the rest of the anthology, this section employs an interview style, focusing on successful Asian Australians who have challenged racial and cultural expectations. The contributors are diverse, from writers and comedians to politicians and corporate advisers. Their lives may have taken varied paths but, as in the other sections of the anthology, there are common threads running throughout the experiences they recount.

### Leaving Home

This section focuses on the experience of reconciling internal and external perceptions, and developing a clear sense of self. The stories are often quite painful and detail the transition from childhood and a state of dependence to adulthood and independence. As in 'The Folks', several stories deal with the conflict between parental expectation and individual desire, but there is also a focus on attempting to reconcile the cultural conflict within oneself, and to establish a sense of place and identity.

### Homecoming

The anthology concludes with a section exploring what it means to discover a sense of home, whether that be through a physical or a metaphorical journey. For some writers, the experience of visiting their ancestral homeland provides a connection to an important part of their identity, whereas for others it merely exacerbates existing feelings of dislocation and a lack of belonging.

# BACKGROUND & CONTEXT

Pung's anthology covers a broad period of time, touching on historic migration in the nineteenth century right through to the final years of the twentieth century. The majority of the stories focus on the post–World War II years, as Asian migration expanded significantly and Australia moved towards a policy of multiculturalism.

While racial, cultural and linguistic diversity are common features of contemporary Australia, it is important to understand that this has not always been the case. In order to understand the issues encountered by many of the writers and their families, some knowledge of Australia's historical approach to Asian migration is useful, along with an understanding of the social and political environment in the final decades of the twentieth century.

Asian migration to Australia has a long history, dating back at least as far as 1818, but it is only in relatively recent years that this migration has involved consistently significant numbers. Government policy restricted the immigration of non-Europeans until the early 1970s, but since then there has been a steady influx of people from a variety of Asian countries. Asian migration is typically classed as the third wave of migration, following a wave from the United Kingdom and northern Europe in the 1950s, then from southern Europe in the 1960s.

Since 1990, Asia has provided more than 50 per cent of Australia's net permanent settlers; in the 2016 census, 12.25 per cent of the population claimed one of the top six Asian ancestries (Chinese, Indian, Filipino, Vietnamese, Korean and Sri Lankan).

## Early migration and the gold rush

The first significant migration of Asians into Australia occurred from the late 1840s, when indentured labourers were brought to Australia to help address the labour shortage that had resulted from the virtual cessation of convict transport. More than 3000 Chinese workers arrived in Sydney between 1848 and 1853, largely to work in agriculture in New South Wales. Further, and more extensive, migration to Australia occurred in the following decades, with the discovery of gold in Victoria prompting a rush of Chinese migrants. During the 1850s and early 1860s, around 40 000 people – overwhelmingly males – undertook the three-month voyage to Australia, leading to Chinese migrants accounting for 3.3 per cent of Australia's total population in 1861.

Local reactions to both of these migrations were resoundingly negative: in Sydney, there were protests about the indentured workers, and in Melbourne, restrictions on Chinese migration were introduced by the Victorian parliament. This anti-Chinese sentiment was predominantly due to fear of competition on the goldfields, as well as opposition from the trade unions over migrants' willingness to work for lower wages. Riots occurred in both Victoria and New South Wales as a result of this unrest.

Following the decline of the gold rush, Chinese populations in the goldfields fell, with many relocating to the cities. Anti-Chinese sentiment increased in Melbourne and Sydney. Fear of migrants was seen as a driving force in the push for federation (in which the states joined together to form the Commonwealth of Australia), as it would enable the government to take a cohesive approach to border control and keep out Asian migrants. Propaganda of the time sought to demonise the Chinese, portraying them as opium-addicted, smallpox-carrying criminals.

## The White Australia policy

Australia's federation in 1901 also saw the beginnings of the White Australia policy, which sought to restrict immigration to those of British and European ethnic origin. One of the first pieces of legislation passed by the new Australian government was the *Immigration Restriction Act 1901*, which enabled immigration officers to exercise discretion regarding who to admit to Australia. While it was not explicitly racial in nature, it allowed for the use of a dictation test that could be administered in any European language of the immigration officer's choice. This meant that, in practice, it was used to prevent non-European migrants settling in Australia.

The White Australia policy was supported by successive Australian prime ministers across the first half of the twentieth century, with many stating explicitly that Australia needed to be 'kept white' and maintain the 'purity' of its national character.

The policy continued for some years following World War II, as Australia was concerned about its vulnerability to attack from countries within the Pacific region. While Australia embarked on an aggressive immigration campaign to increase its population, it targeted British and European migrants. This led to a significant influx of British, Italian, Greek and Dutch migrants, along with smaller numbers from other Southern and Central European countries.

During the 1950s, Australia began to relax restrictions around the policy as it sought to increase immigration. Towards the end of the decade, the *Migration Act 1958* abolished the dictation test and introduced a visa system similar to the one that exists today. Further amendments to the immigration system in 1966 allowed greater access for non-European migrants, particularly refugees from the Vietnam War, and enabled migration opportunities for qualified and skilled workers, who were viewed as being able to contribute to Australia's economy.

The White Australia policy formally ended in 1973, when all provisions regarding race were removed from immigration law, meaning that all migrants, regardless of origin, were entitled to the same entry and settlement conditions.

## Post-1970s migration

The abolition of the White Australia policy and the coinciding political turmoil in several Asian countries led to a significant increase in Asian migration to Australia from the 1970s onwards. Refugees from the

Vietnam War began arriving during the 1960s, with a significant influx between 1975 and 1985 as part of a refugee resettlement scheme. Widely known as 'boat people' due to their arrival in Darwin on crowded vessels, they marked the first large Asian community in Australia since the gold rush. In 1971, only 717 people of Vietnamese descent lived in Australia. By 1981, that had increased to 52 299. Elsewhere, the declaration of martial law in the Philippines sparked a surge in Filipino migration, and this was followed by the arrival of many fleeing Pol Pot's regime in Cambodia during the late 1970s and early 1980s.

People of Chinese ethnicity entered Australia as refugees from conflict in Vietnam and Cambodia, followed later by economic migrants from Hong Kong and Taiwan in the 1980s and 1990s. Since 2000, large-scale Chinese migration has occurred due to China's economic development, as people move to pursue business and education opportunities in Australia.

The Colombo Plan, a program designed to develop cross-country partnerships in the Asia-Pacific region, provided opportunities for students from Malaysia and Sri Lanka to study in Australia, with many settling in the country once their studies concluded. Ethnic unrest in the 1980s in Sri Lanka also encouraged migration to Australia. According to the 2016 census, 'Indian' is the second-most-commonly-nominated Asian ancestry, with the country providing predominantly skilled middle-class migration from 1973 onwards, as families came in search of space, opportunities and a new start.

During this time, Australia was officially pursuing a policy of multiculturalism, with a focus on accepting and celebrating people's ties to other cultures and backgrounds. It afforded migrants the right to express their cultural identity, in contrast to the strict expectations of assimilation and integration in earlier decades.

While the dismantling of the White Australia policy afforded Asian migrants the opportunity to come to Australia, it is important to note that hostility and a lack of acceptance within society often remained. In 1988, then Leader of the Opposition John Howard, who would later become prime minister, proposed a 'One Australia' policy that called for an end to multiculturalism and a reduction in Asian migration. This was followed in the mid-1990s by the rise of Pauline Hanson and her One Nation party, which campaigned aggressively – and often in openly racist terms – against multiculturalism and in favour of the preservation of so-called Australian culture and values.

## Recent challenges

While it can be tempting to look upon many of the attitudes and situations encountered by the writers in *Growing up Asian in Australia* as outdated and belonging to another time, it is important to consider the anthology in relation to the ongoing racial challenges within Australia. The Cronulla riots in 2005 saw predominantly white protesters target Middle Eastern youths, while a series of 2009 attacks on Indian international students in Melbourne led to large-scale protests, with Chinese students expressing similar concerns about their treatment and targeting. In 2020, discrimination against and racially motivated attacks on people of Asian appearance were reported as a result of the COVID-19 pandemic and its perceived origins.

## Australia in the 1970s and 1980s

Some knowledge of the social and cultural context of the late twentieth century will also assist with developing an understanding of the world into which many of the writers found themselves transplanted. While contemporary metropolitan Australian society is diverse and cosmopolitan, things were more homogenous during the 1970s and 1980s, and even more so away from the major cities, in country areas.

Mainstream 'Aussie culture' revolved predominantly around muscle cars, football, pub rock and meat pies. Television shows such as *Countdown* (1974–87) and *Hey Hey It's Saturday* (1971–99) showcased pop music and provided slapstick entertainment, with the latter featuring blackface skits, while Malaysian Australian performer and regular guest Kamahl was often the butt of racist and culturally insensitive jokes. The fact that such content was allowed on mainstream television highlights the prevalent attitudes to racial difference at the time. Some acknowledgement of the changing demographics of Australian society did occur, however, with the launch of the Special Broadcasting Service (SBS) as a radio station in 1978, and its subsequent expansion into television in 1980; the organisation provided programs aimed at ethnic minorities and broadcast in languages other than English.

Sport, a perennially popular Australian source of entertainment, was arguably even more monoracial than the wider society. Few players of Australian First Nations backgrounds were found in any of the major football codes or in cricket, and players of Asian heritage were overwhelmingly absent.

Anglicised versions of Asian food became more widespread in the 1970s, but predominantly consisted of concoctions such as sweet-and-sour pork, beef with black bean sauce and lemon chicken, rather than authentic traditional dishes. Indian spice mixes such as Keen's and Clive of India became more common, as Australian home cooks became more 'adventurous' in their cuisine, but traditional home-cooked meals consisting of 'meat and three veg' were enduringly popular.

Moreover, traditional ties to the United Kingdom were still strong, with 'Advance Australia Fair' only replacing 'God Save the Queen' as the national anthem in 1984.

# GENRE, STRUCTURE & LANGUAGE

## Genre

While *Growing up Asian in Australia* is an anthology featuring a variety of text types, the content can be largely categorised as belonging to the genre of memoir or reflective writing.

Much of the material within the anthology is autobiographical, but the term 'memoir' is more apt because of the limited timeframe of most of the stories. An autobiography or a biography is the story of an entire life, while a memoir focuses on a particular event or time period. Memoir is typically concerned with re-creating events through storytelling, with an emphasis on the use of literary language and on plot, which fits with the pieces in the anthology. The word 'memoir' stems from the French for memory (*mémoire*), and this hints at the subjective nature of memoir compared to autobiography; a memoir tends to focus on the author's subjective recollections, thoughts and feelings about an event more than on its factual accuracy.

The writers in this anthology share their experiences, and those of their relatives, and reflect on how they illustrate the wider experiences of Asians in Australia. This consideration of the meaning and impact of events and interactions places the stories as reflective writing, as the writers seek to explore wider messages relating to identity, society and culture through their recollections.

## Structure

*Growing up Asian in Australia* is divided into twelve sections, each centred on an element or archetype associated with Australian culture, history or rites of passage. By structuring an anthology of Asian experiences around quintessential 'Aussie' traits, experiences and characters, Pung encourages readers to consider the ways in which elements of identity can blend or collide, and the impact on those involved.

'Strine', the opening section, is named after the informal term for Australian English and the Australian accent. It highlights the importance of language – in terms of vocabulary, pronunciation and accent – and the role it plays in both internal and external feelings of belonging and connection.

'Pioneers', 'Battlers' and 'Mates' all relate to celebrated archetypes within Australian culture and ideas of the Australian national character, but they are used subversively. The first title relates to the celebration of the early settlers and the hardships they faced. There is, of course, a level of irony in any reference to pioneers, as the term implies people who were first, and thus disregards the existence of First Nations Australians. And, in a tongue-in-cheek inversion of the notion of pioneers as it is traditionally understood in Australia – as a reference to white settlers – the book makes clear that many Asian Australians were also pioneers, in that they were among the first to migrate to Australia from their homelands. 'Battlers' and 'Mates' are frequently seen as two pillars of the Australian character – the first representing the ability to persevere through adversity and hardship, and the second personifying the qualities of equality, loyalty and friendship that are summarised in the term 'mateship'. While both terms undoubtedly encompass admirable characteristics, Pung encourages readers to question how reflective they actually are of Australian society. The 'Mates' section, in particular, presents a hostile Australia, suspicious of difference and with no sense of equality to be seen.

'The Folks' and 'The Clan' both relate to the concept of family, which has cross-cultural significance. The informality of the former hints at the nature of Australian families, which are characterised by nurture, tolerance and permissiveness, in contrast to the often stricter, less outwardly affectionate Asian parent–child dynamics. The influence of extended family and the associated expectations are explored in 'The Clan', again presenting a contrast between the Anglo-Celtic and Asian approaches. There is an underlying irony in the use of the term 'clan', which has been adopted as an Australian term but has its roots in

Anglo-Celtic history, emphasising how white traditions have been adopted as intrinsically Australian, whereas Asian customs remain inherently foreign.

'Legends' highlights the need for role models, and there is again a tension between the word's literal meaning and its connotations in the Australian vernacular. Here it is used to mean those who are admired, rather than myths or stories of yore, perhaps hinting at white Australia's lack of such a rich cultural history. 'The Hots' relates to romance and – as with many of the section titles – highlights an informality in the Australian approach that contrasts with many of the traditional Asian expectations revealed in the stories.

The title 'UnAustralian?' implies that there is a definitive idea about what it means to be Australian. 'Un-Australian' is a term often used in the media or by politicians to criticise actions or behaviours that are seen to challenge the national identity. In presenting a selection of pieces that deal with ideas about identity and integration under this title, Pung invites readers to question where Asian Australians fit into this definition.

'Tall Poppies' is typically a derogatory term, used to criticise those whose success has led to an inflated ego and who need bringing back down to earth. Pung subverts the term here, using it as the title for a section that highlights the successes of notable Asian Australians across a range of fields. Rather than needing to be 'cut down', these tall poppies should be allowed to bloom and flourish, it is suggested.

The final two section titles, 'Leaving Home' and 'Homecoming', refer to rites of passage and progression. Fittingly, these are the closing sections, as they relate to ideas of transition, maturity and adulthood. With 'Leaving Home', a time often associated with celebration and adventure, Pung again flips the expected narrative, presenting stories of pain and upheaval, encouraging readers to consider the difficulty of leaving 'home' if one isn't sure where one's place actually is. The final section, 'Homecoming', implies a celebration and a return, but deals instead with accounts of dislocation and alienation, building on the uncertainty around the concept of 'home' introduced in the preceding section.

### Story structure

Inevitably, there are a variety of structures within the pieces in the anthology. There are, however, a few recurring examples. Aside from the structural elements identified below, note how many of the stories conclude with a reflection on the events that have been described, either providing an explicit comment on what has occurred or positioning readers to consider the implications themselves.

Given that the majority of pieces are very short, there is little space to establish context and character, so many writers use an opening hook to draw in their readers. This is typically one or two lines at the beginning, which create interest and encourage the reader to continue.

Consider the opening lines of the examples below. What questions do these lines raise? Where could these stories go? Do they make you want to read on?

***Examples:*** 'Perfect Chinese Children', 'The Asian Disease', 'Are You Different?', 'Tourism'.

*In medias res* is Latin for 'into the middle of things'. It is a literary technique whereby the story begins in the middle of the action. The origins are then filled in as the story progresses, typically through the use of flashbacks or description. Several stories employ this strategy to draw readers in and to deposit them straight into the world of the narrative. Given that many writers are relating experiences where they felt bewildered, dislocated or uncertain, this can be an effective tool for inspiring a similar sense of confusion in readers.

***Examples:*** 'Wei-Lei and Me', 'Hot and Spicy', 'Hanoi and Other Homes'.

## Language

Given the variety of material in the anthology, there are many different language features specific to the individual pieces. Here we'll focus on some of the common characteristics of language use in evidence across the anthology.

### Narrative viewpoint

The overwhelming majority of the pieces in *Growing up Asian in Australia* are told using the first-person narrative voice. Given the autobiographical and reflective nature of the stories, this is logical, as it enables the authors to communicate the visceral emotional impact of the events described. It also reinforces the personal nature of the encounters – it prompts readers to remember that these are the lived experiences of real people.

First-person narrative voice also enables a number of writers to explore challenging or confronting experiences with a measure of innocence or ignorance. Given that the focus of the anthology is on events relating to growing up, the protagonists of the stories are often children, and therefore not always able to understand their treatment or the events occurring around them. Some authors explore the thoughts and feelings that eventuate from the experiences, whereas others recount them in less detail, leaving us, as readers, to reflect on the often inappropriate and harsh treatment that these children endured.

### Tense

The majority of the authors use past tense, as they are recounting events that occurred years ago and reflecting on the lessons that resulted. Past tense can also help to create dramatic tension or dramatic irony, as the author or reader may already know that something is about to occur but the characters within the story have yet to discover it. Past tense also allows writers to situate their stories in time and place, encouraging readers to consider the stories as reflective of a wider social and cultural context.

Others present their stories in the present tense, providing a sense of immediacy and helping to create suspense. This enables readers to feel as though they are experiencing the events of the text at the same time as the characters, and tends to encourage readers to make their own assessment of what is occurring – in contrast to those stories written in the past tense, where the author can reflect and evaluate with the benefit of hindsight.

***Examples:*** 'Hot and Spicy', 'Quarrel', 'Baked Beans and Burnt Toast'.

A number of stories in the anthology utilise a combination of past and present tense, drawing on the benefits of both styles. This enables writers to relate an experience, and then, with the change of tense, explore its ongoing effects on them as an adult.

***Examples:*** 'The Relative Advantages of Learning My Language', 'How to Be Japanese', 'You Can't Choose Your Memories', 'The Face in the Mirror'.

### Blended language and culture

The experience of being caught between two worlds or cultures is explored extensively in the anthology, particularly by those writers who are second-generation migrants. Note how they use a combination of Australian and Asian phrases, cultural references and terminology to evoke their experiences vividly and to create a sense of being influenced by two cultures, while feeling fully part of neither.

# SECTION-BY-SECTION ANALYSIS

As an anthology, the text contains a significant number of stories. This guide focuses on one or two from each section of the book, with brief reference to key aspects of the section preceding the detailed analysis.

## Introduction (pp.1–4)

**Summary:** *Alice Pung outlines her intentions in compiling the anthology, and provides history and context in relation to the Asian Australian experience.*

The introduction opens humorously, as Pung recounts her mistaken interpretation of the term 'Power-Points', which was used to describe Asians. This emphasis on the common casual racism expressed towards Asian Australians demonstrates the importance of the anthology as a vehicle for Asian Australians to tell their own stories. Pung also identifies a lack of Asian characters written by Asian authors when she was growing up, positioning the anthology as an opportunity to redress the balance for future generations. She suggests that increasing the visibility of the Asian Australian experience and highlighting its connections to universal adolescent experiences will lead to greater levels of social understanding and acceptance.

You might like to visit Pung's website to read her original, more political, introduction, which provides additional exploration of the key themes of the anthology. (See 'References & reading', p.76.)

### Key vocabulary

*Ancestral*: of, belonging to or inherited from one's forebears.

*Progeny*: descendants or offspring.

## Strine (pp.5–21)

Language is the focus in this opening section, as the authors illustrate the importance of language to connection with others, and the frustrations that language limitations can cause.

### 'The Relative Advantages of Learning My Language' (pp.7–9)

**Summary:** *Amy Choi reflects on her relationship with her grandfather and her renewed interest in learning Chinese following his death.*

Amy's relationship with her grandfather highlights the conflict that often exists between generations. A traditional man, her grandfather 'wrote poetry on great rolls of thin white paper with a paintbrush' and spent his Mondays 'at a large round table at Dragon Boat Restaurant with other old Chinese men' (p.7). While Choi reveals only snippets of her grandfather's life, it suggests a man who is keen to maintain his links to a country he has left behind, and who takes pride in traditions.

By contrast, Amy identifies as Australian and has 'let [her] Chinese go' (p.7). She is immersed in an English-speaking society, and Chinese has no relevance to her – she doesn't 'see the point of speaking Chinese' because 'we lived in Australia' (p.7). This reflects the rejection of culture common to many second-generation migrants as they seek to assimilate into the society in which they live. It also reflects the generational conflict of being a teenager, a period of life when individuals often reject their parents' interests and values as they seek to establish identities of their own.

Amy's renewed interest in learning Chinese is presented as a direct result of her grandfather's diagnosis and death from a brain tumour, and her 'sense of regret' (p.8) at her treatment of him. She highlights the importance of language as a means of connection to family – its human, rather than cultural, significance. Her insistence that she is 'not trying to "discover [her] roots"' (p.9) distinguishes her from other characters in the text, for whom cultural connection is significant.

### Key point

Note the change from past to present tense shortly before the end of the text. Choi uses this change to illustrate the impact of her past experience on her present self.

***Q*** How does Amy's intent in learning Chinese contrast with that of others elsewhere in the anthology? Compare her motivation with Ivy Tseng's in 'Chinese Lessons'. What might this indicate about the different functions of language, and about the relationship between language and culture?

#### 'Sticks and Stones and Such-like' (pp.9–15)

**Summary:** *Sunil Badami reflects on his experience of racism due to being Indian and his struggles with his name.*

Badami establishes a link between names and racism from the opening line, noting that he has 'been called a lot of things' (p.9). Moving into a list of racial epithets, he highlights the casual racism endemic in Australia, where slurs are used 'affectionately' and the safest response is to 'rise over it' and 'take it good-naturedly' (p.9). By moving from these derogatory terms into a discussion of his name, Badami suggests that mispronunciation and an unwillingness to learn unfamiliar names play a similar role in maintaining cultural divisions within society. While initially downplaying the significance of the name-calling, Badami reveals the horrific impact it can have on a child when he details his attempts to 'wash the black off' (p.10) by scrubbing his arm raw.

The story focuses on Sunil's attempts to avoid being viewed as different. His desire to change his name to the more Australian-sounding 'Neil' highlights the adolescent impulse to be one of the crowd, not to stand out. Keenly aware that his skin colour marks him as different, Sunil desires a name that meant he 'fitted in' (p.12).

By presenting his name as unique and special, Sunil's mother succeeds in instilling pride in him about his identity and, by extension, his cultural heritage. This appeals to the flipside of adolescent desire, the need to be different and special. He moves from wanting to be the same as everyone else to feeling 'sorry for Matthews B, C and H' (p.14).

## Key points

Note the blend of Australian and Indian cultural references throughout the story, such as 'if I had a dollar for every time, how many rupees would that make?' (p.10). This is also a feature of other stories within the anthology, highlighting the cross-cultural influences on the writers as they grow up.

***Q*** Why might Sunil's mother take this approach to his name change, rather than telling him off or criticising him? What impact does it have on his feelings towards his Indian heritage? Can you find examples of this gentler approach to cultural conflict elsewhere in the anthology?

### Key vocabulary

*Epithet*: a word or phrase relating to a characteristic of a person, used in place of a name.

*Morning puja*: a morning worship ritual in the Hindu religion.

*Venkateshwara bhajjans*: devotional Hindu songs.

# Pioneers (pp.23–50)

The stories in this section focus on first-generation migrants. While differing significantly in form and content, these pieces suggest that the confusion, dislocation and hostility experienced due to migration transcend time.

### 'The Beat of a Different Drum' (pp.42–50)

**Summary:** *Simon Tong focuses on his language-related challenges, first at an English-speaking Christian school in Hong Kong and then in Geelong after his move to Australia in the early 1980s. He emphasises the importance of rhythm and music to understanding language, as well as the impact language has on one's sense of self.*

Tong explores the intrinsic connection between language and identity, and emphasises the loss of self he experienced due to his inability to articulate his thoughts and feelings in a new language. He experiences this twice: first while still in Hong Kong, when he moves to an English-speaking high school, and again, with greater intensity, following his relocation to Geelong.

The inversion of traditional adult–child relationships is suggested through Tong's description of his journey to Australia with his mother. She is entirely reliant on him to understand and interpret the announcements. Similarly, the middle-aged man in the transit lounge has to ask Tong, a teenage stranger, for help to get his mother something to drink (pp.44–5).

### Key point

Note the connection between language and power and its impact on relationships. While children typically look to their parents for direction and guidance, this story – like many in the anthology – illustrates how the power balance in the adult–child relationship is disrupted due to the language barrier. In many cases, it is the children who have greater language competence, and therefore their parents (or other adults) must rely on them to navigate society.

***Q*** How does Tong show the overwhelming experience of beginning school in Australia? What do the comments by the other boys indicate about non-Asian Australians' understanding of those of Asian background?

#### Key vocabulary

*Duilian*: a couplet in Chinese poetry.

*Sotto voce*: an Italian term meaning 'in a quiet voice'.

*Transpicuous*: easily understood, transparent.

*The Vedas*: religious texts of Hinduism.

## Battlers (pp.51–71)

As the name of the section suggests, these stories focus on those who work hard to establish themselves in tough conditions. Historically, the term 'battler' was often applied to those in rural settings, and that is reflected in this section, where many of the stories relate to Asian Australian experiences in country towns or the outer suburbs of cities.

### 'Take Me Away, Please' (pp.64–7)

**Summary:** *Lily Chan relates the demanding and unrelenting experience of running a Chinese takeaway during the 1980s and 1990s.*

This story simply relates Chan's daily schedule, working in the family business, yet it makes the strain and unrelenting nature of the demands on the young girl clear. An understated story, it presents the Chans as quintessential Aussie battlers, struggling to survive in a sometimes hostile environment, and suggests that their experience is representative of many others. Chan is restrained in her depiction of the demanding schedule she and her family endure, but her desire for something different is clear in both the title and in her acknowledgement that academic success is the only way out.

Chan brings to life the intimate world she grew up in. The Chans' main competitors are also their closest friends, by virtue of shared heritage; they stick together against the 'small, prejudiced town' (p.66). Work and life occur in the same location, with the girls sleeping in a storage area, while homework is done around phone orders. Customers ordering relatively mild dishes such as Mongolian lamb and Singapore noodles are described as 'adventurous' (p.66), emphasising the insular and unworldly nature of the Queensland town.

## Key point

Note how the writing style mirrors the events recounted. Chan employs a sparse, functional style, with minimal description and no wasted words. This suggests both the universality of the experience – it could be any day in any number of years – and the lack of time for frivolity, as she has grown up in an environment where work dominates and nothing is superfluous.

**Q** While the stories differ, what similarities can you identify in the writers' experiences of their parents' businesses and occupations? What does this suggest about the Asian approach to success?

#### Key vocabulary

*Gweilo*: a Cantonese slur, literally meaning 'ghost man', used to describe a foreigner, particularly a westerner.

## Mates (pp.73–100)

School is a formative experience for most young people, and it plays a significant role in the lives of the writers in this section. The desire to belong is a central theme in many of these stories, as difference can lead to ostracism and bullying.

#### 'Wei-Lei and Me' (pp.75–81)*

**Summary:** *Aditi Gouvernel relates her experience of moving from Delhi to Canberra in the early 1980s, the bullying she was subjected to by Barry West, and the confidence she gained from her friendship with fellow migrant Wei-Li.*

The story commences in the playground with a normal game of tag; however, Barry West's extreme response to Aditi being 'it' highlights the racism and ignorance prevalent in Australia at the time, which feeds into the childhood tendency to pick on difference in others. Barry's rejection of Aditi, which she later reveals is repeated by others, is contrasted with the hope and pride her family feel in the move to Australia. They see Australia as 'a place we can make ours' (p.75) and consider their citizenship papers valuable, storing them in the bank vault with the family jewellery.

Gouvernel explores the different meanings of 'becoming Australian', and suggests that a significant gulf exists between becoming a legal

---

* Note that although the story's title refers to 'Wei-Lei', her name is spelled 'Wei-Li' throughout.

citizen and being accepted. She notes that her family 'became Australian in 1982' (p.75), but it is not until many years later, when she is a young adult, that she feels a tangible sense of belonging, as indicated by the final line of the story: 'We had become what we thought we could never be: Australian' (p.81).

Barry the bully is presented as emblematic of white Australia at the time – ignorant, prone to racist stereotyping and suspicious of difference. A caricature in many ways, he is a stock-standard schoolyard bully, fuelled by aggression and horribly violent. There is a delicious irony in his exit from the story, with his move to Jakarta implying a sense of natural justice and the potential for him to become the victim, rather than the perpetrator.

Gouvernel highlights the idea of safety in numbers, and how a desire to belong can lead to unexpected alliances. Her friendship with Wei-Li endures, even though it is borne out of necessity, and their only initial connection is the non-white colour of their skin and their shared victimisation. However, Gouvernel's naming of other characters who join in the bullying – Amy Pulawski and Cris Kovacic – complicates this idea of an alliance of victims. Both characters have surnames that suggest post–World War II migration; the implication is that they could have been past victims of Barry, but their response is to participate in the bullying and thus gain acceptance. By contrast, despite an initial sense of relief when Wei-Li becomes 'the object of their attention' (p.77), Aditi stands up for Wei-Li.

## Key point

The fellow bullies' European surnames hint at the legacy of the White Australia policy, highlighting a country more willing to accept white migrants than those of other racial backgrounds.

***Q*** Where in Australia is this story set? How might the setting add significance to the treatment that Aditi and Wei-Li experience?

**Key vocabulary**

*Dhoti*: a type of sarong or loincloth worn on the lower half of the body by Hindu men.

*Gout*: a form of arthritis.

## The Folks (pp.101–43)

This section centres on parent–child relationships, with particular focus on the challenges that arise due to differing values. The majority feature Asian-born parents and Australian-raised children, but note Mia Francis' reflection on her adoption of a Filipino boy, which flips the narrative.

### 'Perfect Chinese Children' (pp.103–11)

**Summary:** *Vanessa Woods reflects on her challenging relationship with her mother and her failure to live up to her mother's high standards. She relates her experience of growing up as a mixed-race child with divorced parents, and the sense of dislocation she felt as a result of not completely fitting in to either culture.*

Woods explores the differences in expectations between Chinese and Australian cultures, highlighting that although behaviours might be the same, the expected response is not. While Chinese marriages are no more idyllic than Australian ones, 'saving face' is paramount, and therefore 'no one divorced' (p.105). Her mother is left financially and emotionally impoverished by divorce, her loss of face compounded by the comparative averageness of her children compared to those of her relatives.

The story focuses on stereotypical expectations, with much discussion of how success is measured in high marks, financial status, career pathways – particularly becoming a doctor or lawyer – and doing what is expected. Woods offers subtle criticism of these expectations, questioning whether they lead to happiness. Her mother is described as doing 'everything required of a dutiful Chinese wife' (p.105), and yet she still finds herself divorced and destitute.

Vanessa herself is caught in the middle in many ways – both Chinese and Australian, but fitting in to neither culture; she is poor within a wealthy extended family and ambivalent towards education in a world obsessed with academic prowess. She struggles to deal with her mother's tough love, unrealistic expectations and lack of emotional support, while also facing playground racism and isolation. Unable to realise the sacrifices her mother is making, she acts out, but later comes to understand that her mother showed her love through small actions, rather than demonstrations of emotion.

***Q*** Are all the parent–child relationships depicted in this section as fractious as that between Vanessa and her mother? Which would you describe as positive, and which as difficult? Are there similarities in the parenting approaches of those you have grouped together? How have these approaches affected the relationships?

#### Key vocabulary

*Kampong*: a village in Malaysia, Indonesia or Singapore.

*Mahjong*: a tile-based game that originated in China.

*Sinewy*: lean and muscular, with little fat.

## The Clan (pp.145–70)

Building on the exploration of parent–child relationships in the previous section, these stories focus on family in a wider sense. They serve to highlight the importance of family in Asian cultures, and to contrast it with the narrow, nuclear concept of family in Australian society.

#### 'Tourism' (pp.147–52)

**Summary:** *Benjamin Law relates his childhood experiences of visiting theme parks and the layer of significance added to these visits after his parents' separation.*

Law opens by emphasising his family's Asian-ness, contrasting their fear of the outdoors with the Australian love of camping and the beach. He then highlights the marked difference between his family and Asian tourists, recounting how he and his siblings made a conscious effort to appear different from those visiting from overseas. This exploration of where his family fits into society is extended into a discussion of his parents' divorce, which is viewed negatively by the Chinese community, although no one shows real care or concern for his mother. The implication is that the family is caught between Australian and Asian worlds.

Theme parks can be read as a metaphor for the gradual assimilation of the Law family, and perhaps Asian migrants generally, into Australian society. At the prestige Gold Coast parks, the family are initially stuck in the middle – they are not Asian tourists, but the implication is that they have more in common with them than with white Australian residents. The visits to less exciting theme parks that follow Law's parents' divorce can be interpreted as the Law family's gradual attempts to blend into mainstream Australian society. The attractions all have a strongly 'Aussie' element to them – centred around beer or wildlife, for example, as well as a nostalgic park dedicated to Australian history. It is here that Law extends the tourist metaphor – he acknowledges his position as an outsider and observer, a 'tourist' watching other families and contrasting them with his own. The final description of how such 'lesser' theme parks have ceased to exist, coupled with his revelation that the family is considering going camping, points to the societal change that has occurred, with the Law family members now feeling 'Australian' in a way they did not at the story's beginning.

***Q*** Why do Law and his siblings not want to be mistaken for 'actual Asian tourists'? What does this suggest about their sense of identity?

## Legends (pp.171–92)

These stories explore role models and icons that had an impact on the writers when growing up. The importance of family features again, illustrating that Asian Australians must often look close to home for inspiration, perhaps due to a lack of successful role models in wider society.

**'Destiny' (pp.176–9)**

**Summary:** *Shalini Akhil relates her childhood obsession with Wonder Woman and her grandmother's gentle manipulation of this hero worship that enables Shalini to incorporate elements of her Indian heritage.*

Akhil's story focuses on the importance of role models and the ways in which they help children form a sense of identity. Her grandmother is presented as an astute and kindly influence, supportive of Shalini's aspirations but acutely aware of the differences between the young Indian girl and her white idol. By identifying the attributes of Wonder Woman that Shalini admires and putting an Indian spin on them, the grandmother achieves what many older relatives in the anthology fail to – inspiring a genuine sense of cultural pride and engagement in a younger generation. Akhil suggests that, by focusing on the young girl's interests rather than on seemingly outdated traditions, her grandmother makes Shalini's Indian heritage relevant to her and fosters in her a sense of pride in her cultural background.

## Key point

Like Sunil Badami's mother, Akhil's grandmother presents Indian culture in a positive way, allowing Shalini to develop a sense of pride in her heritage. This enables Shalini to be inspired by a role model who is a combination of Indian and Anglo influences, blending cultures, rather than presenting them as diametrically opposed.

***Q*** Three stories in this section discuss the relationships between the writers and their fathers. How do each of the writers depict their relationship with their father, and are the relationships described similarly or differently? What do the writers admire about their fathers?

### Key vocabulary

*Bête noire*: a French term meaning 'black beast', used to refer to someone or something that one particularly dislikes.

*Capacious*: roomy, having a lot of space inside.

## The Hots (pp.193–222)

The development of a sexual identity can be a difficult part of any adolescence, and the stories in this section illustrate how cultural expectations and norms can add another layer of complexity to an already challenging time.

### 'My First Kiss' (pp.216–19)

**Summary:** *Lian Low reflects on the challenges of navigating her sexuality, having been born and raised in a Malaysian society with strict anti-homosexuality laws, while also dealing with other elements that mark her as an outsider.*

Low presents the challenges one faces when an outsider on multiple levels. Moving to Australia, she finds herself grouped with other Asian students socially and academically, on the basis of her recently arrived status rather than her actual linguistic capabilities. Already aware of her sexuality, she struggles with shyness even after making friends, feeling acutely conscious of her accent and its difference.

The pop culture references date Low's adolescence to the early 1990s, adding another layer to her inability to discuss her sexuality with others. Even after leaving Malaysia, Low kept her sexuality secret, as many quarters of Australian society were intolerant of homosexuality. Identifying as a fan of one of the few openly gay celebrities of the time, such as k.d. lang, was often used as a coded way to indicate sexual preference.

Ultimately, this is a story of growth, and Low celebrates how creativity has given her the opportunity to explore and refine who she is. Low depicts herself as struggling to reconcile her multiple identities and the external perceptions that come with them; however, unlike some others in the anthology, Low appears to have the support of her family as she navigates this.

## Key point

Note that Low focuses on the internal in this story – it is about her own perception of belonging. She reveals little about how others behave towards her, in contrast to other stories about migrant high-school experiences.

***Q*** Based on your reading of this section, what are some commonalities in Asian societies' attitudes towards sexual expression? How does Xerxes Matza's experience in 'The Embarrassment of the Gods' contrast with this? Does this make things easier or more challenging for him than for writers such as Low or Benjamin Law?

#### Key vocabulary

*Philandering*: frequently entering into casual sexual relationships; typically used in reference to men.

*Scoliosis*: a lateral curvature of the spine, often occurring during puberty.

## UnAustralian? (pp.223–50)

This section, perhaps more than any other in the anthology, addresses cultural conflicts and the challenges of 'fitting in'. Note how a number of the stories, rather than focusing on the writers' internal feelings, address the societal response to Asian Australians, indicating the prejudicial attitudes that are rife within Australia.

#### 'Anzac Day' (p.239)

**Summary:** *James Chong recounts his brief brush with fame as a teenage bagpiper and the conflicted feelings of belonging that resulted.*

In one of the shortest stories in the anthology, Chong explores the conflicted feelings he experienced as an Asian Australian teenager, unable to feel a true sense of belonging to his adopted country. Much of the story's impact lies in the public humiliation that James receives at the hands of the ABC, Australia's national broadcaster. After detailing his pride in participating in a parade that represents the essence of

Australianism, Chong's revelation that even the national broadcaster questions his place in the commemorations presents a damning picture of Australia and its values.

Chong's account highlights the racism and hypocrisy inherent in celebrations of what it means to be Australian, and makes clear that, traditionally, being Australian essentially means being white. The story opens with a quote from Brendan Nelson that positions John Simpson Kirkpatrick as a quintessential Australian, yet Simpson – like James Chong – was born overseas. Bagpipes, another imported element, are seen as part of the Anzac tradition, but Chong feels excluded because of his skin colour. These observations are presented without irony – there is no questioning of whether bagpipes or Simpson belong, whereas it is clear that Chong, despite his pride and respect, does not.

***Q*** Compare James Chong's story with Uyen Loewald's poem 'Be Good, Little Migrants'. What do both suggest about Australian society's attitude towards migrants?

### Key vocabulary

*Cheong-fun*: a Cantonese rice noodle roll.

*Kawaii*: a Japanese word meaning 'cute'.

*Vestige*: a trace or remnant of something.

## Tall Poppies (pp.251–83)

This section differs considerably from the rest of the anthology, taking an interview format as various Asian Australian public figures are asked to respond to a series of questions. Each entry provides a brief introductory biography of the subject, followed by questions about their aspirations, influences and experiences.

While the fields in which the subjects work differ vastly, all express a similar sense of determination and a drive to succeed. Most also reference their families' attitudes towards their chosen career path. As in many other stories in the anthology, some interviewees received the unconditional support of their family, whereas other families were initially more ambivalent.

***Q*** What is implied by Hoa Pham's use of the word 'now' in her comment 'my mother and father are now really proud of me' (p.263)? What does this suggest about her parents' perception of her career path?

## Leaving Home (pp.285–315)

The title of this section has both a literal and metaphorical meaning, addressing both the departure of the writer or protagonist from the family home and the transition from adolescence to adulthood.

### 'Five Ways to Disappoint Your Vietnamese Mother' (pp.287–91)

**Summary:** *In a humorous story with sad undertones, Diana Nguyen presents her fractured relationship with her mother in the form of a list outlining the ways that she has failed to conform to her mother's expectations.*

Nguyen highlights the hypocrisy in her mother's behaviour by opening with a recount of her piano and ballet lessons as a child. While Diana's mother is happy to revel in the reflected glory of her daughter's successes when Diana is young, she becomes frustrated when Diana continues her study of arts and humanities, viewing it as a distraction from more valuable academic pursuits. Nguyen emphasises the hypocrisy of her mother's belief that Diana's comparatively poor school results make her lose face while she is unable to see that her choice to repeatedly leave midway through Diana's performances has the same effect on Diana.

The story is a cautionary tale of the dangers of imposing strict rules and expectations on the next generation. Diana is presented as well-rounded, balanced and content – she 'had a fulfilling school experience' (p.287), works four jobs and is 'still with [her] boyfriend after five years' (p.291). By contrast, her mother is depicted as superficial, prejudiced and narrow, entirely responsible for the failure of the relationship.

### Key point

Note the phrasing when Nguyen discusses language – she refers to Vietnamese as 'her [mother's] language' (p.289). This highlights the difference between Nguyen's view of herself as Australian, or Vietnamese Australian, and her mother's continuing perception of herself as solely Vietnamese.

***Q*** The stories in this section describe challenging relationships with parents and the pressure of their expectations. What similarities can you identify between the parents of Diana Nguyen, Pauline Nguyen and Paul Nguyen? How have their expectations affected their children?

#### Key vocabulary

*Filial obedience*: respect for, and submission to, the decisions and values of one's parents.

## Homecoming (pp.317–40)

The title of the anthology's closing section is both literal and metaphorical, interrogating the concept of home. The writers invite readers to consider different ideas about what constitutes home, and whether it is physical or more linked to a feeling of belonging.

#### 'Baked Beans and Burnt Toast' (pp.329–37)

**Summary:** *Jacqui Larkin recounts starting primary school, followed by her first visit to Hong Kong many years later, where she encounters a surprise from her past.*

By transitioning between her arrival in Hong Kong as an adult and her first day of primary school, Larkin illustrates her repeated sense of being an outsider, caught between two worlds. While she may fit in appearance-wise in Hong Kong, her inability to speak Cantonese marks her as an outsider and is a source of amusement to the customs officers; in contrast, on starting primary school her command of English is strong but her appearance marks her out as different, particularly in the eyes of her teacher.

Through these experiences, Larkin suggests that prejudice and stereotyping is, to some extent, universal. Mrs Barton immediately focuses on Jacqui's differences from the other students. Her comment 'welcome girls and boys. You too, Jacqui Soo' (p.332) positions Jacqui as a distinctive addition to the classroom, not one of the class like the others. Her assumption that Jacqui has limited English and must have been born overseas reflects an Australia unfamiliar with Asian migration. Larkin, however, shows herself to be equally guilty of pigeonholing when she imagines Peter Nugent's future as 'a walking stereotype with a beer gut' (p.334), as are the customs officers she encounters at Kai Tak airport.

The story's central revelation – that Larkin's waiter was once the boy who teased her in primary school – provides a sense of hope, inviting readers to consider their own assumptions about others, in the same way that Jacqui must. Having previously considered Peter representative of the 'ugly face' of Australian racism (p.334), her discovery that he is more at home in Hong Kong, her supposed home, emphasises the importance of not judging people on face value or appearance.

## Key point

This story explores the universal nature of prejudice – both white and Asian characters are depicted as guilty of making assumptions about others based on their appearance.

***Q*** Compare Larkin's experience of visiting Hong Kong with Blossom Beeby's return to South Korea. What are the similarities and differences in the way they feel and how they are treated? How does this affect their sense of self?

### Key vocabulary

*Epicurean*: relating to pleasure derived from food or drink.

*Hangeul*: the Korean alphabet.

*Hodge-podge*: a confused mixture.

# CHARACTERS & RELATIONSHIPS

The anthology does not feature consistent or recurring characters, but there are certain figures who appear in various guises throughout the text.

## Children/adolescents

**Key quotes**

'I felt at times, though, that because of my heritage and the colour of my skin, I was not allowed to be part of the Anzac tradition, which to many people defines what it is to be Australian.' (James Chong, p.239)

'To this day I am to some extent confused ... am I more Asian or Australian?' (Michelle Law, p.245)

The central character in most of the pieces in the anthology is a young person, often the writer themselves. In many cases, they are depicted navigating a challenge or situation relating to their experience of growing up, usually involving cultural conflict.

These protagonists are frequently presented as outsiders who experience a sense of alienation and a lack of belonging. This can be due to a range of factors, including ethnicity (Sunil Badami, Aditi Gouvernel, James Chong), language competence (Simon Tong), family expectations (Vanessa Woods, Diana Nguyen, Pauline Nguyen), being biracial (Vanessa Woods, Joo-Inn Chew, Leanne Hall), sexuality (Benjamin Law, Xerxes Matza) or cultural disconnection (Amy Choi, Blossom Beeby).

Many of the adolescent characters have a conflicted understanding of self and they struggle to come to terms with their own identity. The writers present the familiar internal conflict of adolescence, of trying to figure out who one is and where they fit, but illustrate how it can be compounded by cultural and racial factors for those with a different background from the majority in the society in which they live.

The reflective quality of these stories, which look back at adolescence from the vantage of adulthood, enables the writers to chart their journey from innocence to experience, as the characters develop a greater sense of understanding about events or a more mature perspective on the behaviour of others. Initially, the central character may not fully comprehend what is happening to them, even if the reader does. Events are often presented in a child-like, simplistic way, such as Amy Choi 'wishing [she] was white or Aussie ... and doing Little Athletics or watching TV' (p.18) without understanding her father's motivations for teaching them Chinese, or Vanessa Woods' desire for 'erasers with Snow White on them' (p.110), which her mother can't afford. But by the story's end, the significance and impact of the events is clear to both narrator and reader.

## Parents

### Key quotes

'... we had the chance to witness our parents' struggles during their first years in Australia, and so to understand them better.' (Diem Vo, p.158)

'Even at nine o'clock in the morning the humming of industrial sewing machines could be heard and would continue being heard until the early hours of the next morning.' (HaiHa Le, p.169)

Given the book's focus on growing up, it is no surprise that parents feature prominently in the anthology. Their qualities, their relationships with each other and their relationships with their children are all explored at various points in the text.

Parents are generally depicted as hard-working and determined to provide a better future for their children. Many of the parents featured run their own businesses, which consume almost all their time, and their children function as additional employees outside school hours. There is often a focus on material provision over emotional support, with many parents appearing distant and detached, even though their care for their children is shown in the commitment to provide for them.

There are common traits in the depiction of parents across the anthology, highlighting the commonalities in the Asian Australian adolescent experience.

### Fathers

#### Key quotes

'Dad was up before we were awake and didn't finish work until late at night.' (Ray Wing-Lun, p.92)

'Liang Liang, you will make our Pan's family very proud one day.' (Cindy Pan's father, p.179)

'He's my dad. And I want to grow up to be just like him.' (Chin Shen, p.185)

'He had never attempted to get to know or understand his children. What assumptions he did come up with were based on anger and venom in his heart.' (Pauline Nguyen, p.294)

Fathers feature prominently in the anthology, with a number of stories exploring the relationship between the writer and their father. For some writers, their father is a distant figure, referred to only in passing, as he is consumed by work. Others are emotionally absent due to traumatic experiences prior to arriving in Australia. Fathers in the anthology largely fall into one of three categories: the disciplinarian, the support figure and the sick or dying. There is also some crossover between the groups.

The disciplinarian father has exacting standards and pushes his children – often to extremes. Pauline Nguyen presents the strict regime under which she was raised, with any grade below an A resulting in physical punishment, noting that 'fear dominated every day of my childhood' (p.292). Similar expectations around academic and financial success are hinted at in 'The Water Buffalo' and 'The Year of the Rooster', where distance has grown between a child and their father due to the incompatibility of their aspirations and values.

Other writers, however, portray more positive versions of fathers, with some touching depictions of intimacy. Unlike the disciplinarian who drives his children to success through fear, Cindy Pan's father inspires her through positivity, vocalising his belief in her capabilities. Pan's warm depiction, just like Chin Shen's loving and humorous description of his father's eccentricities, contrasts starkly with the fearful figure in Pauline

Nguyen's story, highlighting that while an authoritarian approach may yield material success, the emotional cost is great.

Ill and dying fathers appear in several stories, with writers reflecting on their father's life and their relationship with him. The pieces have similarities in their depictions of a once proud and seemingly formidable man brought low by illness, and the challenge of having to confront their father's mortality. However, they vary in their depictions of the father figure himself. 'The Asian Disease' and 'The Year of the Rooster' present the most positive images of a father and his successes, while 'The Water Buffalo' and 'Conversations with My Parents' contain some elements of positivity, but the legacy of the father's past authoritarian approach is shown to colour his relationship with his children.

## Key point

Note that the stories do not address the death of any mothers, hinting at the patriarchal structure of traditional Asian families and thus perhaps the greater reflection inspired by the loss of a father.

### Mothers

## Key quotes

'To my mother, I was the slut daughter. I am still with my boyfriend after five years and I'm still a slut in her eyes. I guess I will be for the rest of my life.' (Diana Nguyen, p.291)

'She said that she was working hard to give me everything I wanted. Money as love. I wanted a mother, not an ATM.' (Paul Nguyen, p.297)

Like fathers, the depictions of mothers in the anthology tend to fall into distinct categories. Fiercely aspirational mothers who have demanding expectations of their children are depicted, but there are also a number of positive maternal role models.

The stereotypical 'tiger mum' (a strict or demanding mother) is present in a number of stories, and is shown to be every bit as damaging to a child's sense of self as her male counterpart, the disciplinarian father. While the expectations of and pressure from mothers are shown to be just as extreme as those from fathers, there tends to be a greater focus on emotional manipulation from female parents. Vanessa Woods and Diana Nguyen relate how their mothers compared their academic scores to those of their friends or relatives, questioning why they didn't do as well as or better than them, leaving both girls with a sense of inadequacy and failure. Paul Nguyen experiences emotional abuse when he reveals his sexuality to his mother and she asks, 'how could you do this to me?' (p.300) and 'why do you want to hurt me so badly?' (p.301), before later announcing that she considered suicide but didn't follow through only because of her patients. While some writers, such as Vanessa Woods and Paul Nguyen, understand their mother's motivations to a degree, for others, such as Diana Nguyen, the emotional damage permanently affects the relationship.

In other stories, mothers are presented as nurturing and caring, showing genuine warmth and affection towards their children. In 'Exotic Rissole', both Tanveer Ahmed's mother and his friend Lynchy's are depicted positively, emphasising the universal aspects of motherhood, while Francis Lee's account of his mother's quiet heartbreak at his departure for Australia is touchingly restrained. Mothers are often depicted expressing concern about their children's behaviour, or about the social outcomes of situations. In many stories they are in the background, often preparing food, quietly supporting in a secondary role.

### Relationships between parents

**Key quotes**

'My parents fought a lot too, but they seemed to have no problems staying together.' (Tanveer Ahmed, p.98)

'Chinese spouses had affairs, slept in separate rooms and barely spoke to each other, but no one divorced. It was a matter of saving face.' (Vanessa Woods, p.105)

Parent relationships are touched on in a number of stories, especially when the relationships are turbulent or fraught. This exposes cultural values and expectations around marriage, with a number of writers referencing the shame of divorce or separation. The importance of maintaining face is highlighted, with the suggestion that keeping up appearances takes precedence over personal happiness. Where separation or divorce does occur, such as in Benjamin Law's 'Tourism', the community's reaction is included, emphasising the perception of divorce as a cultural taboo, and the hypocrisy often associated with that view.

## Parent–child relationships

**Key quotes**

'And in her sacrifice, I see love.' (Vanessa Woods, p.111)

'I am not even sure exactly what words I should use to tell my parents I love them in Vietnamese. I have never told them.' (Oanh Thi Tran, p.131)

Parent–child relationships are often challenging due to inherent generational differences and adolescents' innate desire to establish themselves as individuals. In *Growing up Asian in Australia,* these clashes are often exacerbated by cultural conflict and differing values, since many of the younger generation are born in Australia while their parents are not. The adolescent desire to fit in with one's peers while establishing independence from the family unit can lead to a rejection of traditions and values. Equally, the severe and uncompromising approach to parenting depicted in some stories is shown to be at odds with the more laissez-faire attitude of Australian parents, which exacerbates the resulting conflict.

## Extended family

**Key quotes**

'My dad's parents and his seven siblings owned two rows of double-storey houses on the same street, and family gatherings occurred regularly.' (Diem Vo, p.156)

'… he insisted we head to Sydney because he had brothers and cousins there.' (Ken Chan, p.165)

Other relatives appear frequently in the anthology, illustrating the importance of extended family in Asian cultures. Their depictions highlight differences from white Australian approaches to family. Examples include the isolation Diem Vo's friend feels when her parents are fighting, which Vo cannot relate to because of her huge extended family, or the contrast between Barry, who shares a room with his brother but doesn't have enough to eat or adequate clothes, and Ken Chan, who shares a three-bedroom house with eight adults, but is always well-fed and clothed.

### Key point

Many writers link extended family and parenting. This enables them to contrast the individualistic Australian approach and the collaborative Asian style. Through this, the writers explore the differences in familial values between cultures, suggesting these also significantly impact connection to Australian society.

With parents often absent due to work demands, other family members are shown to step in and fulfil their roles. Some, such as Yee Mah in 'Perfect Chinese Children', are formidable, employing 'emotional terrorism' (p.109) to maintain order, while others, such as Shalini Akhil's grandmother in 'Destiny', use a gentler approach.

Grandparents are present in a number of stories, reflecting the duty of taking care of one's elders. They also represent the 'old country', often having a greater sense of history and connection to tradition than younger family members. This illustrates another challenge of migration, with adaptation shown to be even more difficult for older generations.

## White Australia

### Key quotes

'My mother had warned me, "We have to watch out for *gweilos*. They can be nice sometimes but they won't always treat you the same."' (Ray Wing-Lun, p.91)

'Jamilah migrated to Australia a few years after the White Australia Policy had been lifted, but she understands the bruise of being dark-skinned in Australia.' (Simone Lazaroo, p.119)

'Perhaps he's just the face – that ugly face – of all those Aussies who've enquired, "Why don't you go back to where you came from" down the years.' (Jacqui Larkin, p.334)

Overall, white Australia is not depicted positively in the anthology. It is presented as narrow-minded, prejudiced and, at times, violently racist. This is an accurate reflection of Australia during the later decades of the twentieth century, when the legacy of the White Australia policy lingered and multiculturalism was in its infancy. Many of the challenges the writers face stem from the prejudice and preconceptions with which they are confronted.

The school playground often reflects wider attitudes within a society, as children learn their views from their parents but are more direct in expressing them. A number of writers in the text feel they 'met Australia in the school playground' (p.76). Some bullies, such as Barry West, have distinct identities, while others are depicted as an anonymous, amorphous mob, such as the one that confronts Simon Tong with a barrage of names on his arrival at school, or the 'playground wits' (p.10) who torment Sunil Badami. The torrent of abuse so many writers face makes clear the extent of the prejudice aimed at Asian Australians. Yet, while the playground is predominantly presented as confronting and hostile, some bullies also show the prospect of redemption. Peter Nugent, Jacqui Larkin's tormenter in 'Baked Beans and Burnt Toast', is later depicted as fluent in Cantonese and working in Hong Kong, which he reveals is due to his youthful fascination with the writer during primary school. Such outcomes hint at the possibility of a more inclusive Australia.

In the text, the adults in Australian society are frequently portrayed as prejudiced and unwelcoming, albeit often in more subtle ways than children. Simone Lazaroo illustrates the systemic racism in Australia through her depiction of the prejudice shown by police and nurses who interact with her father. While the police are outright racist in 1968, the nurses' attitude towards Lazaroo's father decades later in the final stages of his life is perhaps even more shocking, and highlights the lingering nature of racial and cultural stereotypes in Australian society.

Such casual racism and prejudice are depicted throughout the anthology, and are shown to have a significant impact. Sunil Badami recounts how the racial epithets came from parents as well, while

Mrs Barton's exclusionary attitude to Jacqui Larkin on her first day of primary school exacerbates Jacqui's existing feelings of difference. The effects of stereotyping are also illustrated, with Leanne Hall recounting her experience of labels such as 'Asian' and how these impacted on her identity. Through these characterisations of white Australia, the writers highlight the cumulative effects of racism and its prevalence across all sectors of society.

Although negative depictions are common throughout the anthology, white Australians are not portrayed exclusively as hostile and prejudiced. Some writers explore their friendships with white peers, or the assistance they received from white Australians. Lynchy in 'Exotic Rissole' is presented as a stereotypical Australian, but his friendship with Tanveer Ahmed is shown to be warm and honest, despite their starkly different backgrounds, while Simon Tong's friend Stewart is patient and non-judgemental regarding Simon's linguistic mistakes. When there are hints at a broader positive societal attitude, such as in 'The Asian Disease', it tends to be illustrative of a later time period, implying changing attitudes over the years – though even then it may be couched in disappointment.

## Key point

Positive depictions of white Australia tend to be of individuals, as opposed to of groups, implying that the prevailing attitude within Australian society is a hostile one.

# THEMES, IDEAS & VALUES

## Identity

### Cultural identity

**Key quotes**

'… I still found it hard to tie my Indian appearance to my Australian feeling (eventually settling for an awkwardly knotted hyphen to make me Indian-Australian or Australian-Indian, depending on the day) …' (Sunil Badami, p.14)

'I am Australian. I am a second-generation Australian Vietnamese. My mum would stress that I am Vietnamese-Australian. All my life I've had this mixed idea of who I am and what my role is.' (Diana Nguyen, p.289)

'No matter where I am it seems as though I will always be caught in the middle … I'm East meets West, an ABC, a banana.' (Jacqui Larkin, p.331)

Many of the writers struggle to define themselves culturally, and to work out where they fit into conflicting cultures. This is shown to be particularly true of second-generation migrants, who have been born and raised in Australia, and whose connection to their Asian culture is only through their parents and grandparents. Due to the desire to 'fit in' and be like everyone else, many reject the culture of their parents, as they seek to be 'Aussie'. The reflective conclusions to many stories explore a sense of regret about this rejection, or a belated interest in previously dismissed traditions. There is a sense that generational differences are compounded by culture, often resulting in an irreparable schism between parents and children.

First-generation migrants experience different challenges regarding cultural identity. Language, traditions and beliefs are ways to maintain a connection to their country of origin, but this has to be balanced with fitting into a new, unfamiliar and often hostile society, which has little understanding of the environment from which they have come.

Those who are adopted experience further challenges with cultural identity and often feel even more unsure of where they fit. Blossom

Beeby and Mia Francis reveal that their parents were advised 'not to acknowledge Asian-ness' (p.324). For Beeby, in particular, this leads to a conflicted sense of self, as she is convinced she 'would eventually evolve into a fully-fledged Caucasian' (p.324) because of the white, monocultural world of her upbringing. Bereft of a connection to their birth culture, adoptees can struggle to establish a clear sense of self.

### Sexual identity

**Key quotes**

'I discovered that boys liked me, and that entirely changed my self-image.' (Jenny Kee, p.220)

'Promise me that you'll stay straight until twenty-four, then afterwards you can do whatever you want.' (Paul Nguyen's mother, p.301)

The development of sexual identity is explored in a number of stories, particularly in 'The Hots' section of the anthology. Both heterosexual and homosexual writers recount the challenges they faced in adolescence, illustrating the blend of repression, taboo and expectation that accompanies sexual expression across a range of Asian cultures. While their backgrounds differ, the writers relay a shared experience – heterosexuality was mandated, marriage was expected and pre-marital sex was frowned upon for girls. A daughter who didn't adhere to these expectations, or who was perceived as not doing so, risked being accused of being 'nothing more than a common whore' (p.294).

The writers who share their experiences of coming to terms with their homosexuality reveal the narrow stereotyping within Australian society that pigeonholes people into distinct groups, rather than considering them as multifaceted, complex individuals. As Benjamin Law explains, 'people never suspected you could be a racial minority *and* gay' (p.200).

### The role of appearance

**Key quotes**

'It was a surprise and a contradiction. To feel at home in a place because of my appearance, without being able to feel the connection between the person I am and the way I look.' (Leanne Hall, p.234)

'When we looked at our faces in the mirror, though, foreigners would appear.' (Blossom Beeby, p.324)

Appearance is shown to play a significant role in the confused sense of self that several writers experience. Trying to negotiate others' judgements based on outward appearance adds to the sense of dislocation and loneliness explored by many writers. This may manifest in the realisation that one may never look like one's role model, as Shalini Akhil experiences in 'Destiny', or in a narrow perception of what constitutes beauty, as indicated by Hoa Pham 'drawing [herself] with blonde hair and blue eyes, because that was how [she] wanted [herself] to be' (p.261). While many of the writers come to embrace their Asian Australian identity over time, for others this is depicted as an ongoing journey.

## Language

### Language and identity

**Key quotes**

'Robbed of speech again, but this time both inside and outside the classroom, I was stripped of my dignity and personality as well.' (Simon Tong, pp.47–8)

'If I couldn't express myself, then who was my self?' (Simon Tong, p.48)

'My attempts to blend in failed as soon as I opened my mouth.' (Lian Low, p.217)

As well as enabling communication, language is a tool for self-expression, and it is through language that others come to know us. Several writers in the anthology explore the loss of identity that can occur when language competence is low, revealing the impact this can have on a person's self-esteem. Simon Tong relates feeling 'robbed of speech, hearing and literacy' (p.44) even before leaving Hong Kong, due to moving to a high school where all classes are taught in English. He transforms from being 'an attentive and conscientious student' who 'won the school's essay competition every year' (p.43) to one who 'didn't make a peep in class' (p.44). This is exacerbated once he moves to Geelong, where he is treated 'like a child' (p.48), ultimately leaving him with uncertainty around his sense of self. This highlights the challenges faced by teenage Asian Australians, particularly first-generation migrants, as they negotiate the ordinary difficulties of adolescence and establishing a sense of self along with the additional burden of limited expression and infantilisation from others. Even Lian Low, for whom English 'was the language [she] spoke in, dreamt in and created [her] reality in', felt like 'a foreigner whenever [she] opened [her] mouth' (p.217), illustrating the importance of language and expression in identity construction.

### Connection to family, culture and heritage

**Key quotes**

'Maybe these lessons were also a way to ensure that his three Australian-born and bred daughters recognised that their Chineseness was not restricted to their black hair, small round noses and consumption of rice. Theirs was deeper, a heavier inheritance of over 4000 years of history, language and values.' (Ivy Tseng, p.18)

'My lack of interest in learning her language created a lasting communication barrier between me and my mother.' (Diana Nguyen, p.289)

The role of language in maintaining a link to culture is crucial, particularly across generations. With younger generations more likely to have a higher level of English competence than their parents, and their parents and grandparents likely to speak the ancestral language more fluently, a gap opens between the generations. Many second-generation migrants in the anthology display a reluctance to learn the language of their parents or grandparents because it seems irrelevant: they 'spoke English all day at school, listened to English all night on TV' (p.7). The significance of the cultural links language affords often isn't appreciated until the writers are older, by which time it is too late for some. Amy Choi admits to not being 'particularly kind to [her] grandfather' (p.7), and it is only after his death that she experiences 'regret' (p.8). While frustration at the perceived outdatedness of one's grandparents is not culturally specific, Choi highlights how language can create another barrier between generations, resulting in even wider gulfs than in monolingual families.

For first-generation migrants, language represents an opportunity to maintain a connection to history and heritage. As the quote opposite about Ivy Tseng's father illustrates, many migrants were keen for their children to understand where they came from, and the associated history of their parents' country. In contrast to Amy Choi, who is only interested in communication, Tseng recognises that her limited Mandarin has had an effect on her sense of self, and wonders if greater fluency would enable her to 'feel more authentic' (p.21).

While not as widely referenced, the importance of popular culture in language learning is also touched on, particularly by Tom Cho and Simon Tong. Both illustrate that learning English is a more complex process than merely understanding the words used, and highlight the important role of cultural understanding. For both writers, and others elsewhere in the anthology, television plays a part in helping their language development. Cho's chaotic and nonsensical story highlights the role of popular culture, and hints at the need to establish cultural, as well as linguistic, understanding when attempting to fit into a new country.

### Language as a tool for connection

**Key quotes**

'I am simply trying to ensure that the next time an elderly relative wants me to listen to them, I am not only willing, I am able.' (Amy Choi, p.9)

'"I'm sorry," I reply tersely. "I don't speak your language."' (Jacqui Larkin, p.335)

The absence of language can have a profound effect on one's ability to interact with others. Ivy Tseng fantasises about having parents who can speak perfect English, rather than 'standing awkwardly to one side, smiling, at school functions' (p.18) – wanting to participate, but unable to due to the language barrier.

Some narrators are excluded from languages other than English, illustrating the multiple levels on which Asian Australians can experience cultural and linguistic exclusion. Jacqui Larkin recounts the embarrassment of not understanding the question 'do you speak Cantonese?' at Hong Kong airport (p.330), while Michelle Law stumbles over ordering an ice cream at McDonald's in Hong Kong (pp.244–5), highlighting that assumptions about a person's linguistic competence are made in Asia as well as in Australia. This emphasises the disconnect that many Asian Australians experience, 'caught in the middle' (p.331) of two cultures.

Those who have a command of several languages can use language to include or exclude others. Amy Choi addresses her brother in English because she thinks her grandfather won't understand, seeking to deliberately leave him out (p.7). Other writers note that exclusion can be self-imposed. Diem Vo observes that her parents 'found it far easier to deal with other Vietnamese-Australians than to learn English', but that 'this kept them alienated from the non-Vietnamese-speaking world' (p.158). This common tendency to socialise in communities based around a shared language is presented as understandable but limiting, as it impedes involvement and acceptance in a new culture.

## Belonging

### The powerful need to belong

**Key quotes**

'I didn't feel "black" anything. I just wanted to fit in.' (Sunil Badami, p.10)

'I had never felt alienated by Australian culture, but I was certainly aware of not fitting in.' (Michelle Law, p.244)

The desire to be part of a community is an innate human need. It stretches back to the dawn of civilisation, where being part of a group provided physical safety and improved chances of survival. Even today, with the threat of predators significantly reduced, humans are drawn to others, with the desire for connection particularly strong in young people. The American psychologist Abraham Maslow identified belonging as a fundamental element in his hierarchy of needs, positioning it after basic physiological and safety needs. He suggests that the need to belong and be accepted by others is a key motivator for humans and that, without it, loneliness, social anxiety and depression can have a significant effect on people's lives.

Establishing oneself within a group is part of the adolescent developmental process, linked closely to the development of personal identity. In many of the stories in the anthology, characters attempt to find their place and battle with a sense of not being like everyone else. Those who are biracial often feel a heightened sense of rejection, lacking a true feeling of connection to either Australian or Asian groups.

### Stereotypes, preconceptions and prejudice

**Key quotes**

'Jolly Asians bring nothing but disease. Your life will be a disaster if you marry one of them ...' (Simone Lazaroo's grandmother to Simone's mother, p.113)

'Although we were still sometimes insulted in the streets of our suburb, even spat upon, young Australian men and old ladies stopped my sister and me in the shopping centre and told us that we were beautiful.' (Simone Lazaroo, p.118)

'You Asians are all the same.' (Diana Nguyen's customer, p.289)

Stereotypes and generalisations feature prominently in the anthology, with many writers challenging simplistic notions of what an 'Asian' or an 'Aussie' is. Such stereotypes are often shown to be damaging, as they provide a limited idea of how a person should be, which can then lead to rejection if the reality doesn't match the expectation. This rejection can come from a social or cultural group, or the individual being stereotyped may decide that they do not or cannot fit into the group.

In *Growing up Asian in Australia*, much of the stereotyping relates to appearance, due to preconceptions about how people will behave based on how they look. In 'The Asian Disease', Emanuel Nazario's dark skin means that when he suffers from a disease that makes him slur, the assumption is that he has limited English, even though he has spoken English since childhood (p.119). When Jacqui Larkin begins primary school, her teacher assumes – erroneously – that she was born overseas and has limited English due to her Asian appearance. Jacqui is already conscious of being 'the only Asian kid in the school' (p.332), and her teacher's comments further exacerbate her sense of difference. James Chong's 'Anzac Day' reveals stereotypical judgements taken to a new height, with the ABC questioning his participation in an Anzac Day parade on national television (p.239). Through such examples, the writers illustrate that exclusion is not always overt, but even when it is exercised in more subtle ways, it can have the same corrosive effect. None of these individuals experience direct rejection, but the assumptions made about them based on their appearance hinder their ability to feel a sense of belonging. This is especially true for Chong, who espouses the quintessential values of what it means to be Australian, and yet is still left with 'a lonely feeling of exclusion' (p.239).

At times, prejudicial assumptions based on a person's appearance manifest in abuse and violence. Simone Lazaroo's father is 'slammed face-first against the supermarket wall' (p.116) by two police officers who accost him due to the colour of his skin, while juvenile bullies such as Barry West dish out vicious racial slurs and violence in the playground. While Barry's behaviour is shocking, he represents the failings of white Australia more broadly, as his behaviour, attitude and vocabulary has clearly been modelled for him by others. Notably, there is no mention of any punishment for him – which is also the case for Sunil Badami's tormenters in 'Sticks and Stones and Such-like', even when the taunts lead him to scrub his skin raw in an attempt to 'wash the black off' (p.10). Badami's revelation that the racial slurs come not only from 'playground wits' but 'sometimes their parents too', delivered with 'an *affectionate* chuckle' (p.10), points to the endemic nature of casual racism in Australia. These writers present a critical view of white Australia, illustrating the challenges Asian migrants face as they attempt to find connection and belonging. The suggestion is that, regardless of how willing migrants are to embrace Australian values and customs, others' prejudicial treatment imposes limits on their ability to feel a true sense of connection.

### Feeling caught between two cultures

**Key quotes**

'Bronnie and I never quite blend in, but our new playmates are always too polite to mention it ...' (Vanessa Woods, p.106)

'We were half-half, and for a long time we didn't belong anywhere.' (Joo-Inn Chew, p.248)

'It has taken some time for the different bits of me to fit comfortably, and I am sure they will continue to realign and I will continue to question.' (Blossom Beeby, p.329)

The anthology explores the difficulty of belonging when one feels caught between two different identities. Joo-Inn Chew notes that she and her siblings 'didn't seem to belong anywhere' (p.247), as they have little in common with their classmates at their country primary school, but are equally dissimilar to their Malaysian cousins. After a spate of racist taunting in the playground, Vanessa Woods' cousin Erica gives her 'a sideways look, as though she is seeing me for the first time, realising that I look more like one of *them* than like her' (p.107), and Vanessa feels ashamed that she and her sister 'don't even look Chinese' (p.105). Both writers express a sense of disconnect and disorientation, but Chew suggests the potential for belonging if one can find one's place. She details joining the Bendigo Chinese Association and learning 'Chinese dancing' (p.249), and the sense of pride that develops from celebrating a shared connection. Unlike Woods, who struggles to fit in, lacking a connection to others who share her experiences, Chew and her siblings are able to find joy and acceptance in being celebrated 'for being the kind of Chinese that [they] really were' (p.250). Thus, the anthology highlights the importance of connection, especially between those who feel caught between two cultures.

This sense of not fitting in anywhere is not restricted solely to issues of culture and race. Benjamin Law describes himself as an 'Asian hybrid man-child thing' (p.195), with an odd combination of manly and feminine features. He lists his attempts to be more masculine, before eventually conceding that he has 'given up trying' (p.196). Law, like several writers in the anthology, has developed a sense of self-acceptance, which no longer necessitates trying to fit in with others' predefined notions.

## Family

Family plays a central role in the lives of most young people. It is through family that the majority of people learn who they are, where they have come from and how to make sense of their world. Almost all of the texts in *Growing up Asian in Australia* make some reference to family, with many focused on relationships with relatives and the challenges that exist within nuclear and extended family groups.

### Intergenerational conflict

**Key quotes**

'… we had not been talking for ages because of what he saw as my wayward behaviour (I moved out of home before I was married – gasp!) …'
(Oanh Thi Tran, p.130)

'I had been living out of home for three years, which in itself was a supposed statement of defiance against my mother …' (Paul Nguyen, p.300)

Individuation (the process of forming a stable personality) and the construction of a sense of self are important elements in adolescent development. A young person must move towards relative independence from family relationships as they begin to develop the capacity to operate as a member of adult society.

In many Asian cultures, the family is a central institution around which life is constructed, and this desire to establish independence can result in conflict. Many of the writers in the anthology explore the clashes that result from intergenerational conflict as they attempt to resist or reject their parents' influence. Such tensions often extend into adulthood. Mainstream Australian society, which typically has less stringent expectations around filial piety and is more encouraging of adolescent independence, can serve to exacerbate these tensions.

### Role reversal

**Key quotes**

'"Could you please buy a bottle of orange juice for my mother? She is very thirsty, but I can't speak English …" The pleading in his voice embarrassed me.' (Simon Tong, pp.44–5)

'Our younger cousins have not had to act as interpreters, translating at parent–teacher interviews, explaining every bill, forging their parents' signatures and writing their own school sick-leave certificates.' (Diem Vo, p.157)

The traditional family structure positions those who are older as the purveyors of wisdom and guidance – parents and grandparents pass on the benefit of their experience to the younger generations. Several writers, however, explore what happens when these roles are reversed, and the old must depend on the young for assistance, information and survival. Simon Tong highlights the loss of face that results for some of the older generation: he describes a middle-aged stranger's embarrassment when he is forced to ask the teenaged Simon to buy a drink for his mother because he cannot speak English. Tong observes, 'He thanked me profusely, but didn't look me in the eyes when I handed him the juice and biscuits' (p.45), implying the man's humiliation at having to rely on a child to provide for his mother.

### Family expectation versus personal goals

**Key quotes**

'It is the ultimate aspiration for any Chinese mother to have a child who is a lawyer or a doctor.' (Vanessa Woods, p.107)

'My greatest strengths were art, jazz ballet and athletics … but in Form Three Mum insisted I do maths instead of art, and that was the beginning of the end for me educationally.' (Jenny Kee, p.220)

'Initially, when I told them I wanted to go to radio school, they were like, "What? What for?" They didn't think it was a serious or an easy path to follow.' (Caroline Tran, p.283)

The promise of a better life or increased opportunities is a factor prompting the migration of many Asians to Australia. For many migrants, financial stability and prosperity are of great importance, as they aim to provide for their families and to ensure that their children have stability and security. Often influenced by their own limited opportunities when growing up, many emphasise the importance of education and academic achievement, expressing aspirations for their children to embark on prestigious careers in medicine or law. Some believe that with hard work, anyone can achieve anything, and therefore poor results indicate laziness.

Many writers emphasise the significant weight of family expectation they experienced growing up, highlighting its detrimental impact. In 'You Can't Choose Your Memories', Paul Nguyen outlines 'the uniformity with which [he and his friends] were raised' (p.299), with set expectations about academic achievement, career prospects and marriage, indicating the prevalence of such attitudes within the Asian Australian community. The pressure is constant: Pauline Nguyen observes that 'we aimed high because we had no choice' (p.291), as 'any average result was a failure' (p.292), while Vanessa Woods recalls her mother stating, 'ninety-six isn't 100. If you want to do well you have to try harder' (p.103) in response to a maths result she perceived as below par.

If success is defined as meeting set criteria, it presents difficulties for those who do not, or cannot, meet those conditions. Many of the writers experience this challenge when their personal goals and aspirations do not align with their parents' expectations. Some experience rejection – such as Diana Nguyen, who repeatedly sees her mother walk out of her acting performances, to the point that she no longer invites her. Others rebel against the suffocating pressure: Jenny Kee purposely fails her exams in order to be allowed to leave school, having already become sexually rebellious in response to being denied the opportunity to study art. Even those who initially conform – such as the daughter in Thao Nguyen's 'The Water Buffalo', who gives up medicine to become a painter – experience rejection later in life for such unconventional choices, indicating that parental expectations are lifelong. Through her inclusion of these stories in the anthology, Pung illustrates the lasting damage this narrow view of success can cause to parent–child relationships, and warns readers of the dangers of imposing one's aspirations on the next generation. While these writers have become successful, their achievements have come at a cost, with some familial relationships damaged beyond repair.

It is important to note that many Asian parents depicted in the anthology do not view creative pursuits as worthless; they just do not consider the arts a viable career option. Prowess in musical and artistic performance is admired, but as a sign of mastery and roundedness, rather than as anything more serious. Diana Nguyen's mother gossips proudly about her daughter's childhood achievements in piano and ballet, but is later critical of these pursuits when she realises they might get in the way of her academic studies, stating that they were 'supposed to be hobby, not a job' (p.287). Vanessa Woods' mother sends her and her sister to piano lessons, despite their relative poverty. Woods' mother, like Nguyen's, despairs at her daughters' desires to be an actress and a writer, because she 'can't think of anything less likely to lead to one of us buying her an apartment' (p.108), highlighting the focus on fiscal success and material security above all else.

### Key point

There is often an emotional disconnect between the writers and their parents. Many Asian parents are depicted as showing love through material provision, rather than through physical affection or words. Note how many writers recount struggling to express their feelings to their parents.

## Sacrifice

### Key quotes

'He became a working man and thought, "At least I am safe here," but he knew where he had left his heart.' (Thao Nguyen, p.35)

'And in her sacrifice, I see love.' (Vanessa Woods, p.111)

'We were made acutely aware that he and my mother had fled Vietnam not for their own future but for ours …' (Pauline Nguyen, p.291)

While many of the families depicted in the anthology move to Australia in search of a better life, a number of stories are also imbued with a sense of loss. Through this, the writers suggest that sacrifice is necessary if one wishes to establish oneself in a new country.

Some writers, such as Francis Lee and Thao Nguyen, hint at the pain of leaving behind relatives in the pursuit of opportunity or safety, while others, such as Pauline Nguyen, are aware that their parents have abandoned their country for the sake of their children. There is an emotional toll to these types of sacrifice, involving either guilt and sadness for those left behind, or a sense of debt and duty owed to those who sacrificed for their benefit.

Sacrifice is also necessary for belonging, because fitting in requires a certain degree of conformity to the practices of the dominant culture. For many writers, this translates to rejecting their parents' language and traditions, and their Asian heritage, as the lure of mainstream Australian society wins out. It is often only later in life they realise what they have sacrificed, with Amy Choi and Ivy Tseng both reflecting on the opportunities for family connection lost to them as a result of their rejection of Mandarin. This is also true of writers such as Sunil Badami, who eschews his Indian name for the Anglicised 'Neil', before his mother instils in him a sense of pride in his heritage. Given the challenges that many writers face with fitting in, this sacrificing of cultural identifiers is perhaps understandable, even though it is depicted as damaging to one's sense of self.

### Key point

The anthology also hints at the role mainstream Australian society plays in expecting new migrants to sacrifice their culture and adopt the dominant values and customs. Phrases such as 'why don't you speak English?' (p.35) allude to this. The theme is also explored in Uyen Loewald's poem 'Be Good, Little Migrants', where the various definitions of 'being good' centre on adherence to strict expectations of behaviour.

# DIFFERENT INTERPRETATIONS

Different interpretations arise from different responses to a text. Over time, a text will evoke a wide range of responses from its readers, who may come from various social or cultural groups and live in very different places and historical periods. Responses by critics and reviewers can be published in newspapers, journals and books, both online and in print. They can also be expressed in discussions among readers in the media, classrooms, book groups and so on.

While there is no single correct reading or interpretation of a text, it is important to understand that an interpretation is more than a personal opinion – it is the justification of a point of view on the text. To present an interpretation of a text based on your point of view, you must use a logical argument and support it with relevant evidence from the text.

## The critics' viewpoints

Since its release in 2008, the response to Alice Pung's *Growing up Asian in Australia* has been predominantly positive, with many critics applauding its focus on giving voice to Asian Australian experiences. Reviewers at the time commented on the dearth of such voices in the media, noting that Pung focuses on 'capturing an Australian-ness that is rarely reflected on TV or radio but you'll spot on the train, at schools or next door' (Farouque 2008). It received praise as 'a raw and honest book' that was a 'testimony to the multiplicity of the Asian-Australian experience, too disparate and different to homogenise and label "the other"' (Massola 2008).

The variety of writers and the breadth of experiences captured in the anthology were undoubtedly elements of the text that appealed to readers, but they were also the source of some criticism of the book. James Massola observed that 'the brevity of some of the stories in *Growing up Asian* might lead to charges of an occasional lack of subtlety', with the weighty themes and issues sometimes not given the necessary space to be discussed with complexity. Pung solicited submissions with a general call-out, meaning the content is sourced from both professional and amateur writers, and some critics commented on a variance in the quality of the writing: Farah Farouque noted that 'some of the prose is excellent while other parts more pedestrian' (Farouque 2008). There was, however, praise for Pung's work as editor, collating a 'tightly edited book [that] benefits from the gentle honesty of unique lived experience' (Massola 2008).

The commercial success of *Growing up Asian in Australia*, and its value as a vehicle to give voice to those who have not previously had a platform to speak, is evident in the texts that followed. The anthology was the first of a series of *Growing up… in Australia* books, which now stretches to several titles, covering the experiences of African, Aboriginal, queer and disabled young people as they navigate adolescence.

**Interpretation 1: *Growing up Asian in Australia* presents experiences specific to Asian Australians.**

As Alice Pung states in the introduction, 'these stories show us not only what it is like to grow up Asian in Australia, but also what it means to be Asian-Australian' (p.4). This framing, given at the very beginning of the text, points to the fact that the experiences of Asian Australians are distinct and specific to their community.

The parent–child conflicts explored in *Growing up Asian in Australia* predominantly relate to traditional Asian concepts of family and duty. In many of the parents, readers can recognise the values of Confucianism, which encourages hard work, filial piety, overcoming adversity, honesty and academic excellence. While several of these values are common across the globe, collectively they characterise the belief system of many Asian cultures. Paul Nguyen identifies 'the uniformity with which all of us were raised' (p.299), and the defined expectations to which all were subjected, illustrating the specificity of the Asian Australian experience. Intergenerational tensions arise when Australian-raised children rebel against the fixed, narrow, Confucianist aspirations of their parents. Those who reject parental expectations are viewed as 'going the way of *Australian* children' (p.105), highlighting the gulf between the two cultures.

Like family conflict, racism can be found the world over, and throughout history; however, the prejudice detailed in the anthology is specific to the Asian Australian experience. Given the constrictions of the White Australia policy, which made Asian migration almost impossible prior to the early 1970s, the majority of the stories in the text are set in the final three decades of the twentieth century. These stories therefore depict a specific time and place – an Australia not used to non-white migration, during a period of evolving attitudes towards multiculturalism. Many writers were the first or only Asian student at their school, or belonged to 'the only Asian family in the entire district' (p.61), at a time when sweet-and-sour pork or Australian-style chop suey were considered exotic, and thus many encountered rampant prejudice regarding all aspects of their culture and appearance. While racism undoubtedly still occurs, and people are still targeted for their difference in the playground and beyond, the prevalence and similarity of the events recounted in the anthology indicate a shared experience specific to Asian Australians.

Language and appearance feature prevalently in the stories, and both are distinctive markers of difference. The disparity between the Australian identity many writers feel when growing up and the way that others perceive them based on their appearance is inherently connected to racial and cultural factors. Language can lead to disconnection and alienation in a way that is unique to migrants and their descendants – limited English impedes their involvement in wider society, while limited competence in an Asian language restricts communication between family members, and can affect one's sense of connection to a cultural heritage. Although many Australian parents and teenagers may feel that they struggle to communicate with each other, this is generally not due to the literal absence of a shared language, which can be the case for Asian Australians.

While there is much in the anthology for all readers to relate to, the catalysts for most of the events and emotions described are specific to the cultural background of the writers and the time period in which they are writing.

**Interpretation 2: The anthology explores universal experiences that everyone can relate to, regardless of their background.**

The experience of growing up is shared by all, regardless of geographical location, ethnicity or language. While elements of the experience may differ, the development of a distinct identity, the separation of oneself from the family unit to establish independence, and the desire to find one's place in society are universal. In her introduction, Alice Pung quotes the poet Horace, saying 'change only the name and this story is also about you' (p.1), while also cataloguing the list of 'firsts' experienced during adolescence. The shared nature of these milestones means that the stories in the anthology explore experiences relatable to all, regardless of heritage or culture.

As Pung notes in the introduction, 'growing up is a funny time' (p.1) – a sentiment that many readers would agree with. The rapid physical and emotional changes of puberty, a growing interest in romantic relationships and the desire to be seen as an independent and autonomous figure are not specific to race or culture. Benjamin Law's description of his physical awkwardness as a 'hybrid man-child thing', with 'hands like a well-manicured woman' and 'a baritone voice' (p.195) and Diana Nguyen's recollection of wearing 'big owl-eyed glasses and a brown school uniform two sizes too large' (p.290) will resonate with anyone who experienced physical or sartorial embarrassment at some point in their adolescence.

The development of a sexual identity is also common to all humans, and the anthology explores those trials and tribulations with sensitivity and humour, in ways that are reflective of the wider adolescent experience. While Simon Tong is frustrated that his language skills limit his social interactions, his desire to 'be a suave Don Juan who can amble nonchalantly over to the emerald-eyed girl' (p.48) could just as easily apply to any teenage boy who has found himself tongue-tied in the presence of a girl. Equally, concern over unfashionable haircuts administered by fathers or being 'a self-conscious teenager with Clearasil and pancake make-up concealing [one's] pimples' (p.220) are shared experiences across cultures and generations. Even those who offer their stories of coming out present experiences relatable to queer adolescents of any background – a fear of rejection, a desire not to be seen as different, and potential conflict with one's family.

The prominent theme of family will resonate with many readers, given the influence that family has on most people's lives. Intergenerational conflict, differences of opinion, the shame of divorce and the challenges of dealing with extended family are all explored and, while cultural specificities may be factors in the disagreements, the nature of such tensions will be familiar to most readers. The experience of 'voices, angry and confronting, pierc[ing] the closed door' (p.159) and 'a rotating roster of weekend custody' (p.149) will be recognisable to anyone whose parents separated during their childhood. Similarly, Chin Shen's admiration for his father will resonate with anyone who has ever suffered second-hand embarrassment at their father's actions while still being secretly proud of him. Love, like conflict, has no cultural designation, and therefore the stories of love, pain, support, loss and heroism in the anthology speak to readers everywhere.

While the anthology undoubtedly focuses on the lives of Asian Australians and the challenges they have encountered, the experiences recounted are universal and resonate widely. While the details of the disagreements and conflicts may be specific, along with the nature of the bullying many encountered, the stories are reflective of the wider experience of growing up, regardless of background or cultural heritage.

# QUESTIONS & ANSWERS

This section focuses on your own analytical writing on the text, and gives you strategies for producing high-quality responses in your coursework and exam essays.

## Essay writing – an overview

An essay on a literary work is a formal and serious piece of writing that presents your point of view on the text, usually in response to a given topic. Your 'point of view' in an essay is your interpretation of the meaning of the text's language, structure, characters, situations and events, supported by detailed analysis of textual evidence.

### Analyse – don't summarise

In your essays it is important to avoid simply summarising what happens in a text.

- A **summary** is a description or paraphrase (retelling in different words) of the characters and events. For example: 'Macbeth has a horrifying vision of a dagger dripping with blood before he goes to murder King Duncan.'
- An **analysis** is an explanation of the real meaning or significance that lies 'beneath' the text's words (and images, for a film). For example: 'Macbeth's vision of a bloody dagger shows how deeply uneasy he is about the violent act he is contemplating, and conveys his sense that supernatural forces are impelling him to act.'

A limited amount of summary is sometimes necessary to let your reader know which part of the text you wish to discuss. However, always keep this to a minimum and follow it immediately with your analysis of what this part of the text is really telling us.

### Plan your essay

Carefully plan your essay so that you have a clear idea of what you are going to say. The plan ensures that your ideas flow logically, that your argument remains consistent and that you stay on the topic. An essay plan should be a list of **brief dot points** covering no more than half a page.

- Include your central argument or main contention – a concise statement of your overall response to the topic.
- Write three or four dot points for each paragraph, indicating the main idea and evidence/examples from the text. Note that in your essay you will need to *expand* on these points and *analyse* the evidence.

### Structure your essay

An essay is a complete, self-contained piece of writing. It has a clear beginning (the introduction), middle (several body paragraphs) and end (the last paragraph or conclusion). It must also have a central argument that runs throughout, linking each paragraph to form a coherent whole. See examples of introductions and conclusions in the 'Analysing a sample topic' and 'Sample answer' sections.

**The introduction establishes your overall response to the topic.** It includes your main contention and outlines the main evidence you will refer to in the course of the essay. Write your introduction *after* you have done a plan and *before* you write the rest of the essay.

**The body paragraphs argue your case** – they present evidence from the text and explain how this evidence supports your argument. Each body paragraph needs:

- a strong **topic sentence** (usually the first sentence) that states the main point being made in the paragraph
- **evidence** from the text, including some brief quotations
- **analysis** of the textual evidence, with **explanation** of its significance and how it supports your argument
- **links back to the topic** in one or more statements, usually towards the end of the paragraph.

Connect the body paragraphs so that your discussion flows smoothly. Use some linking words and phrases such as 'similarly' and 'on the other hand', though don't start every paragraph like this. Another strategy is to use a significant word from the last sentence of one paragraph in the first sentence of the next.

Use key terms from the topic – or synonyms for them – throughout, so the relevance of your discussion to the topic is always clear.

**The conclusion ties everything together and finishes the essay.** It includes strong statements that emphasise your central argument and provide a clear response to the topic.

Avoid simply restating the points made earlier in the essay – this will end on a very flat note and imply that you have run out of ideas and vocabulary. The conclusion should be a logical extension of what you have written, not just a repetition or summary of it. Writing an effective conclusion can be a challenge. Try using these tips:

- Start by linking back to the final sentence of the second-last paragraph, rather than leaping to your main contention straight away – this helps your writing to flow.
- Use synonyms and expressions with equivalent meanings to vary your vocabulary. This allows you to reinforce your line of argument without being repetitive.
- When planning your essay, think of one or two broad statements or observations about the text's wider meaning. These should be related to the topic and your overall argument. Keep them for the conclusion, since they will give you something 'new' to say but still follow logically from your discussion. The introduction will be focused on the topic, but the conclusion can present a wider view of the text.

## Essay topics

1. 'Being different makes it difficult to fit in.' Discuss, with reference to at least three stories from *Growing up Asian in Australia*.
2. 'The experiences recounted in *Growing up Asian in Australia* show us that migration can be both challenging and rewarding.' Do you agree?
3. 'The writers in *Growing up Asian in Australia* struggle to find a balance between conflicting cultures.' Discuss.
4. 'Belonging is vital to human wellbeing.' To what extent does *Growing up Asian in Australia* show this to be true?
5. '*Growing up Asian in Australia* invites the reader to reflect on what it is to be "Australian".' Discuss.
6. How do the writers in *Growing up Asian in Australia* utilise language and stylistic features to convey their personal experiences?
7. 'Sacrifice is necessary if one wishes to belong.' To what extent is this true of the stories in *Growing up Asian in Australia*?
8. 'Cultural differences can present challenges for an individual.' How do the writers explore this idea in *Growing up Asian in Australia*?
9. 'Family can be a source of both comfort and unhappiness.' Discuss.
10. 'Despite the cultural background of the writers in the anthology, the stories suggest that the experiences of adolescence are universal.' To what extent do you agree?

## Vocabulary for writing on *Growing up Asian in Australia*

***Anthology:*** a collection of pieces by various authors, usually in the same form, focused on the same period or the same subject.

***Assimilation:*** the process of adopting, or being forced to adopt, the language and culture of a dominant group or society. Prior to the 1970s, and arguably well beyond this, it was expected that migrants – and First Nations Australians – assimilated into white Australian culture.

***Cultural dissonance:*** a sense of confusion, unrest or conflict experienced by people undergoing change in their cultural environment.

***Culture:*** the behaviours and beliefs characteristic of a particular group of people, as a social, ethnic, professional or age group.

***Ethnicity:*** a social group that shares a distinctive culture, religion, language or background.

***Multiculturalism:*** the encouragement of different cultures or cultural identities in a unified society. From the late 1970s onwards, Australia officially pursued this policy.

## Analysing a sample topic

**'Being different makes it difficult to fit in.' Discuss, with reference to at least three stories from *Growing up Asian in Australia*.**

This topic may appear straightforward, but it is deceptive. It is a good example of an exam-style topic – accessible to most students, but with an underlying complexity. With a topic such as this, it is particularly important to consider each word carefully, and to think about the different opportunities to shape your answer.

Begin by turning the topic into a question, which will help you formulate a contention. Put simply, this topic asks: *does* being different make it difficult to fit in? Your answer to this question will form the basis of your contention. Remember that your response needs to be based on your knowledge and understanding of *Growing up Asian in Australia*, rather than generally. Given the content of the anthology, it is likely that you will agree that it does make it difficult, at least to some degree.

The next step is to interrogate the topic, breaking it into its constituent parts and considering the different directions from which you could approach it. Begin with the phrase 'being different'. In what ways can someone be different? Who or what are they different from? Who determines that they are different? Then consider the phrase 'makes it difficult' – and note the use of the word 'difficult'. This implies that it is not impossible, even though it may be very hard. This gives you more options to form your argument, as you can choose to argue that it is difficult *to some degree*. Finally, consider what it means 'to fit in'. Remember that 'fitting in' often refers to a group, and that groups can be different sizes – for example, family, a friendship group, a gender identity, or society as a whole.

Note the breadth of this topic – the wording does not limit you to discussing race or culture. This gives you the opportunity to consider a wide variety of differences explored by the writers – for example, Benjamin Law's feelings regarding his masculinity and physical appearance. While race and culture are likely to feature strongly in any essay on *Growing up Asian in Australia*, look for opportunities to explore other ideas as well, to show a comprehensive understanding of the text.

Having unpacked the different elements of the topic and generated some ideas, consider how best to organise your arguments. You could, for example, decide to focus on types of difference and how they have an impact on a sense of belonging. Alternatively, you could focus on the different groups into which the writers attempt to fit, and how difference affects belonging in particular contexts.

In the response outlined below, the contention supports the statement, but argues that belonging is also still possible.

### Sample introduction

> Humans are social animals by nature, and, as such, we naturally desire to be part of a community. This idea is explored by many of the contributors to Alice Pung's anthology *Growing up Asian in Australia*, as they recount their experiences of trying to find their place in their families, friendship groups and a sometimes hostile Australian society. The text suggests that being different from others can make it hard to belong, with stories exploring how difference affects both others' responses to an individual and one's own sense of self, resulting in disconnection from others. Hope is conveyed by some of the stories, suggesting that while it may be difficult to fit in when different, it is not impossible.

### Body paragraph outline

**Body paragraph 1:** Appearance plays a significant role in fitting in, affecting one's ability to accept oneself, as well as to gain acceptance from others.

- Consider differences in appearance and the challenges they add to fitting in.
- Discuss how looking different from the majority causes challenges due to others' negative responses. Examples: bullying in 'Wei-Lei and Me' and Sunil Badami in 'Sticks and Stones and Such-like': 'I didn't feel "black" anything. I just wanted to fit in' (p.10).
- Explore how feeling different from how one looks causes difficulty belonging. Examples: Blossom Beeby ('when we looked at our faces in the mirror, though, foreigners would appear', p.324) and Leanne Hall ('I'm like a perpetual toddler batting away at my reflection in the mirror, unable to comprehend that what I see is myself', p.233).

**Body paragraph 2:** Desiring or valuing different things can negatively impact one's ability to belong, leading to rejection or to a feeling of exclusion.

- Focus on behavioural differences and how they can limit belonging.
- Differing expectations within families cause fracturing. Examples: Diana Nguyen, whose desire to be an actor and romantic relationship damage her relationship with her mother, and Pauline Nguyen, who is unable to remain in her family and runs away due to the behaviour of her father.
- Sexuality can cause a sense of alienation. Examples: Benjamin Law, who feels disconnected from his male peers due to his physicality and sexuality, and Xerxes Matza, who feels disconnected from his family due to his failure to 'demonstrate any prowess with either dick or dollars' (p.215), which is what his family values.

**Body paragraph 3:** Fitting in is based on finding connections with others, and many factors contribute to this.

- Discuss the potential for belonging, despite difference. Examples: Aditi Gouvernel and Wei-Li's friendship is based on safety ('when we were together, we felt safe', p.79) and deepens over time; Joo-Inn Chew notes that 'we weren't all friends, but when we stepped out together to the music we were a tribe' (p.249).
- Explore how second-generation migrants feel a sense of connection and belonging when visiting Asian cities, despite often lacking language: 'instead, I felt something I had never experienced before ... acceptance' (p.244).

### Sample conclusion

Throughout the anthology, the writers explore the numerous challenges of adolescence and establishing one's place within society. Many encounter difficulties with fitting in; appearance and behavioural differences contribute to these challenges and impact both the writers' views of themselves and others' responses to them. The anthology does, however, present hope, suggesting that it is possible to find connection, even for those who are, or feel, different from the majority. Through the varied experiences shared, the writers encourage readers to persevere through difficult periods, suggesting that the passage of time can lead to maturity and changing values, thus enabling people to eventually find their place.

# SAMPLE ANSWER

**'The writers in *Growing up Asian in Australia* struggle to find a balance between conflicting cultures.' Discuss.**

Culture is defined as the behaviours or beliefs of a particular group of people, often based on a shared background or ethnicity. In Alice Pung's anthology *Growing up Asian in Australia*, a number of the writers discuss the challenges they experienced growing up under the influence of both Australian and Asian cultures. Differences in family attitudes and concepts of success make it difficult for some of the writers to find balance, but the text also includes examples of cultural stability. Thus, while the writers do struggle with conflicting cultures, they show that achieving balance is possible.

Many of the writers find the different family expectations between Asian and Australian cultures difficult to navigate. The traditional Asian expectation that individuals, particularly girls, will remain at home until they marry can be a source of tension for those raised in a more liberal society. In 'Conversations with My Parents', Oanh Thi Tran reflects on the challenges of trying to meet her parents' expectations while also being true to herself. She recounts the discord with her father due to 'what he saw as [her] wayward behaviour', as she had left the family home before marriage, and notes that sitting with him in hospital is 'one of the few ways I could express that I was a dutiful daughter, even though my values were not his'. Tran's love for her parents is clear, but she evidently struggles to conform to their expectations regarding filial piety, and ponders how to tell them she loves them, as she is 'not even sure exactly what words [she] should use … in Vietnamese'. Paul Nguyen has also moved out early, in 'a supposed statement of defiance against [his] mother', and he highlights the impact of this conflict on his identity, noting that he has 'spent much time trying to define [himself]', and considers himself 'culturally bipolar', having been subjected to his mother's rigid expectations. Nguyen and Tran both illustrate the difficulties of trying to find a middle ground between the fixed family values of their parents' culture and the relaxed attitude of the country in which they were raised, emphasising the negative impact this has on their relationships and their own sense of self.

Conflicting concepts within different cultures around what constitutes success also present some writers in the anthology with challenges, as they struggle to strike a balance. In many Asian cultures, success is measured by academic achievement and financial status, as both are viewed as leading to stability and security, whereas Western culture places more value on pursuing one's interests and 'being happy'. For writers raised in Australia with Asian parents, the disparity between their parents' aspirations for them and their own is frequently shown to lead to conflict. Both Vanessa Woods and Diana Nguyen relate their mothers' disappointment in their desire to pursue careers in the arts, highlighting medicine as the ultimate career goal. Woods' mother 'can't think of anything less likely to lead to one of [them] buying her an apartment', while in Nguyen's mother's eyes she is 'a disappointment'. While Woods is eventually able to recognise the good intentions behind her mother's tough approach, Nguyen's relationship with her mother appears damaged beyond repair. She recounts her mother's repeated rejection of her acting career, along with her labelling of Nyugen as 'the slut daughter' because of her relationship with her boyfriend. While there is humour in the story, the use of a five-step list as a structuring technique reflects the rigidity of Nguyen's mother's expectations, and the vignettes below each step expose the emotional damage resulting from seemingly benign actions such as becoming an actor or getting a boyfriend. While the Australian influence on Woods is explicit, given that she is biracial, it is clear that Nguyen is also affected by the culture in which she has grown up, as the events she relates – school performances, working in a supermarket and getting a boyfriend – are easily identifiable as typical of Australian adolescence. Both women, who have experienced success in their chosen creative fields, illustrate the damaging effects that conflicting cultural definitions of success can have on relationships and on a young person's self-esteem, and warn of the dangers of imposing rigid career or academic expectations upon one's children.

However, while many of the stories explore the difficulties posed by conflicting cultures, the anthology also offers a glimmer of hope by suggesting that balance can be achieved. Several writers indicate that encouraging acceptance of both cultures and attempting to blend the positive elements of each can lead to balance. This is shown in Shalini Akhil's story, 'Destiny', which explores her childhood obsession with Wonder Woman. Her grandmother is less than enamoured of Wonder Woman's outfit, and is also conscious of the racial differences between Shalini and the superhero. Rather than rejecting her granddaughter's role model, the old woman strategically blends traditional elements of Indian culture with the positive, crime-fighting aspects of the Wonder Woman character. By the end of the story, Akhil reveals that Shalini has altered her future goal, and intends to be 'Indian Wonder Woman' when she grows up. Sunil Badami's mother takes a similar approach when her son wants to change his name to Neil, in an attempt to appear less Indian. She concocts an elaborate story regarding the unique origins of his name, which inspires him to feel proud of it. Badami reveals that 'even if I still found it hard to tie my Indian appearance to my Australian feeling … I didn't worry so much about my name anymore … I knew what it meant, and what it meant to my mother'. He instead feels 'sorry for Matthews B, C and H', illustrating that standing out can be a good thing. Even though Badami's mother's explanation is revealed as a lie at the story's end, it has achieved its goal, instilling a sense of pride in her son about his Indian heritage and showing how his Indian identity can coexist alongside his Australian identity. Both Badami and Akhil suggest that balance comes from making room for two cultures, and encourage readers to look for the similarities and the positives, rather than the differences and the negatives. The anthology's inclusion of stories with hopeful outcomes illustrates the potential for seemingly conflicting cultural identities to coexist within an individual.

The battle to balance conflicting cultures looms large over many of the writers in the anthology, and presents a challenge that some cannot overcome. The variety of stories illustrates the difficulties that culture can cause, particularly affecting the self-esteem of those growing up under the influence of multiple cultures. Through presenting the experiences of those who succeed in finding a balance between conflicting cultures, as well as those who fail, Pung highlights the importance of give and take, and the need for compromise and acceptance in order to find cultural equilibrium.

# REFERENCES & READING

## Text

Pung, A 2008, *Growing up Asian in Australia*, Black Inc., Melbourne.

## References


### Books and journal articles

Chakraborty, MN & Walton, J 2020, 'Asian Australian Identities: Embodiments and Inhabitations', *Journal of Intercultural Studies*, vol. 41, no. 6, pp.667–76.

Geldard, K; Geldard, D; & Foo, RY 2019, *Counselling Adolescents: The Proactive Approach for Young People* (5th ed.), Sage Publications, London.

Graham, P 2013, 'Alice Pung's *Growing Up Asian in Australia*: The Cultural Work of Anthologized Asian-Australian Narratives of Childhood', *Prose Studies*, vol. 35, no. 1, pp.67–83.

### Newspaper articles

Farouque, F 2008, 'Growing up Asian in Australia', *The Age*, 24 June.

Massola, J 2008, 'Asian voices add to the great chorus', *Canberra Times*, 6 August.

### Websites

Alice Pung's website featuring the original introduction to the anthology, https://www.alicepung.net/for-teachers-and-students/

The Asian Century Institute, https://www.asiancenturyinstitute.com/migration/214-asian-migration-to-australia

The Cultural Atlas, an educational resource providing comprehensive information on the cultural background of Australia's migrant populations, https://culturalatlas.sbs.com.au/